Max...

Content Promotion,
Podcasting and Advocacy

The Explained! Pocketbook

Steven Christianson

Henley Point
Toronto

Maximizing Content Promotion, Podcasting and Advocacy: The Explained! Pocketbook

By Steven Christianson

The Explained! Pocketbook is a compaction of modified content from the three component publications of the *Explained!* series, also by Steven Christianson.

Published by Henley Point
Toronto, Canada
www.henleypoint.ca

The information contained in this publication is provided for informational and referential purposes only, and should not be construed as legal advice on any subject matter.

Neither the publisher not the author is responsible for websites (or their content) that are not owned by the publisher or author.

Cover design by Josée Scalabrini and Henley Point Productions.

ISBN: 978-1-7778347-5-3

CONTENTS

About *Explained!*   i

About *The Explained! Pocketbook*   iii

Book I   1

   Content Creation and Promotion   3

Book II   105

   Podcasting   107

Book III   193

   Advocacy   195

References and Further Reading   315

ABOUT *EXPLAINED!*

The *Explained!* series was born from a need to find compact, conversational and instructive material that was up-to-date, comprehensive and readily available to just about anyone.

The first book in the series, *Content Creation and Promotion*, was originally released in February 2021. *Content Creation and Promotion* was written to explain how to enhance brand position, organizational personality and overall image, which have become universally important in creating and promoting content. The lessons learned in that book extend beyond traditional product and service marketing, and apply equally to advocacy and social causes, election campaigns and even differentiation of charity organizations. As the book cover conveyed, *Content Creation and Promotion* explains why and how you can reach - and retain - your desired audience.

The second book, *Podcasting*, was published in May 2021 (with a second printing in July 2022), and provides the reader with the technical know-how and requirements of starting a podcast, as well as some history about the medium and how podcasting has grown into an essential component of developing content and depth of brand character. Podcasts and audio technology are also increasingly used to help support and further advocacy goals.

Advocacy (an *Amazon Bestseller*), like the previous two books, implicitly embraces the need and the practice of raising one's voice, of amplifying the message, and of getting that message out there to its intended audiences. The practice and methods of advocacy are about making change, and *Advocacy* guides the reader of a tour of how and where change can be made in lasting and meaningful ways.

ABOUT *THE EXPLAINED! POCKETBOOK*

The Explained! Pocketbook is an extraction of the theoretical precepts contained in *Content Creation and Promotion, Podcasting* and *Advocacy*, while leaving the practical information to the *Companion Handbooks* (stand-alone guides and workbooks published in the spring of 2022). As such, *The Explained! Pocketbook* advances the original objectives underpinning the *Explained* series by offering readers a compaction and modification of the key lessons and reasoning from each of the three books into one compact pocketbook.

The *Pocketbook* is in some ways an anthology of the *Explained!* series. *The Explained! Pocketbook* also explores the broader principles of content, as they apply to audio engagement and outreach, and as they manifest in practice in the processes of advancing social and political change. The *Pocketbook* is divided into three books; and the interrelatedness of each becomes more evident as one recognizes that each Book – indeed, the principles and practices of content creation and promotion, podcasting and advocacy – entail and closely resemble a production. Whether one is immersed in creating visual content, monetizing a podcast, or managing a grassroots advocacy campaign, not only does the work comprise a production, but foundational principles in each are inextricably related.

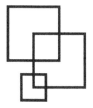

BOOK I

CONTENT CREATION AND PROMOTION

Content Creation and Promotion was written to explain that content today extends beyond traditional product and service marketing, and applies just as importantly to advocacy, social causes, and even election campaigns. This book explains some of the key concepts in identifying and reaching a desired audience. *Content Creation* is about the message. A collection of reflections, Book I is based on a series of podcast episodes published during 2020 and 2021.

CONTENT CREATION AND PROMOTION

1

Your breakfast cereal has a personality. Your insurance carrier speaks with an accent. Your airline has a family history. And so they should. Personifying your product or service can give it a life of its own, separate from the business organization that designed and sells it.

The art of promoting something really boils down to creating that "thing" that people can identify with and relate to.

There is a reason why insurance agents plaster their personal photos all over their promotional materials (such as lawn signs, media ads or profile cards). It builds personality, which can build trust. The public persona of an actor is often quite different from who that person really is. The politician who runs for election, appears before the media commenting on such and such an issue, or plasters his or her promotional materials all over the place, but is usually not the same person as one would experience in private. Personal privacy is something we usually want to protect and share with only those who are close to us. The most compelling reason, though, rests in the ability to construct something more ideal, more sanitized and less fallible, something easier to control.

We all do it to a certain extent, whether we realize it consciously or not: when we build an online profile, with a personal image and a resume of our experiences, we "touch up" here and there, adjusting everything in the visual presentation, from lighting to skin complexion; we try to find the strongest possible words to communicate our job titles and responsibilities, making sure they cater to the audience - the potential employer.

Some people refer to this practice as the art of bullshit. But is it really so bad to put your best foot forward when presenting something, especially if we hope to make a lasting, positive impression?

Of course, there is a clear difference between someone who claims to have a university degree, when in fact that person only attended a few classes. There is a difference between "beefing up" and utter fabrication.

The art of creating content and promoting it, be it a product we designed, a service we offer, or our very selves, is something we all do.

But if someone is different in public than that person is in private, aren't we dealing with fabrication? Isn't the content we create a falsehood? A television commercial about an airline might depict a family member flying off to reunite with other family members. While the family is part of the fiction, that piece of fiction is presented as an example. The commercial needs to personify that example of what the airline offers, otherwise it is unlikely that viewers would relate to the product. So, there is an element of fiction, but one that is based on the very real products and services offered by the company, and one that virtually anyone who is able to buy an airline ticket can see himself or herself fitting right into the scenario depicted.

A key part of promotion is personification. An equally key part is the need for promotion to speak to larger concepts. Let's again consider the example of an airline company. We've probably seen at least one commercial of an airline company. What do they claim to be doing, as the commercial depicts family members reuniting with others? The company isn't just flying people from one place to another; the company is helping to bridge the distance of family members, to help connect loved ones, which then creates stronger bonds and familial relations within that family. It's a broader concept of not only what the airline does, but the impact it makes. And we've seen that impact many times: family members embracing the new arrival at the airport, with hugs and tears of happiness and joy. This is what the airline contributes to; this is the product and service it provides.

So, we always want to remain mindful of the need to personify things as well as the strengths of broadening the concepts associated with what we do.

Of course, if everyone did exactly that, we would have limited product comparison. Imagine if every airline company touted its service as one that "brings families closer", there would be very little differentiation from one to the next. Which is why knowing what you do, who you are trying to recruit into your orbit of sight, and how you are different from others is always a critical first step – and an ongoing, periodic point of self-reflection. Airline ABC might bring families closer, while Airline XYZ might be geared more toward offering cut-rate fares, no-frills service and shorter flights. Two very different narratives of content; two very different forms of promotion.

Content creation and promotion are increasingly valuable tools in today's global, hybrid marketplace that features a combination of e-commerce and bricks-and-mortar, and can be essential skills for just about anyone trying to make a difference in his or her respective field of activity.

Bottom line: there should always be a harmony between content and communication. Achieving that harmony begins with appreciating what promotion actually is, and demystifying the notion that you can't do it yourself.

Promotion is about more than just placing an ad, or putting up a sign in a window or in a parking lot. It is about understanding exactly what you want to promote, and appreciating the perceptions that people have about it. With those perceptions come stigma and sometimes misconceptions. Don't ignore these. Embrace these perceptions and stigma, understand them, and grow to love them. These are your barriers, your problems. Without knowing them intimately, you can never begin to know what it is that you are promoting, and just how you intend to speak to - and retain - your target group.

You may want to "beef up" your online profile. You might be in the market for selling your services as an accountant, an electrician, or a virtual event organizer. Or perhaps you have become passionate about advocating for some issue or cause in your community or across the world. Whatever the case, the tools and tips in Book I – at least one tool or tip – will be useful in your endeavors, and hopefully become foundational to mastering your art of content creation and promotion.

2

The following story exemplifies the importance of defining a problem as part of the overall effort of developing a narrative and determining the most appropriate means of promoting its message. The example in this story is about politics, and efforts to promote, persuade and achieve "buy-in" from potential "customers".

For many people who read or watch the news at home, politics is that realm where passion tends overwhelm: personal feelings, likes and dislikes, notions of power and participation. The theatre of politics tends to consume significant segments of the daily news feeds, which then have the effect of "tickling our passions". Whether we love or despise politics, political news tends to be something that many people can relate to, or at least have defined opinions about. One reason for this is that electoral campaign advocacy reaches out directly to voters, attempting to recruit, change opinion and commit to people to action; and much of this is transmitted through media.

Let's step back to the summer of 2020. Donald Trump was still President of the United States. Joe Biden was the Democratic presidential candidate. But in the months leading up to that point, there had many other aspirants wooing support from Democrats. What was so appealing about Joe Biden at that time, and how did that man figure into the Democrats' strategy? Why was Biden a good choice to promote?

Is it possible that the Democrats put partisan-tinged passion aside and looked at the problem – that is to say, *their* problem? If so, what was that problem? The problem, many had argued, was Donald Trump himself, and the fact that he had power. However, the problem was not actually Trump himself, but the issues that his supporters rallied towards, the *motivators*. The Democrats at that time in the electoral cycle seemed to have grasped the basic axiom highlighted in this Book: they embraced the problem, and they crafted an electoral choice that spoke to it rather than first attempting to find a solution.

This can be somewhat confusing, admittedly, so a little contextual explanation is in order.

There's a massive difference among political supporters, the politically engaged and active voter turnout. One person might have said that he supported Mr. Trump, but then doesn't turn out to vote. That's a supporter. You might find someone who is active and engaged, say, as a volunteer on the phones or canvassing at the doors. That someone could be anyone, a tentative or potential supporter who is curious and wants experience, or someone who doesn't have citizenship to vote but can play an active role in a campaign. Both the supporters and the engaged are critical to any election campaign. But Election Day is what the campaign is all about, and that's where the tally of voter turnout makes or breaks a campaign and a candidate. Who are the people who bothered to leave the house, stand in line, and cast a ballot? And why did they bother to do that?

Those two questions are fundamental, and they should be asked during every electoral cycle (which is really a cycle of promoting content, as well as advancing dialogue around issues and causes). The Democrats seem to have asked those questions: What motivates a Trump supporter? What compels that person to physically get out of the chair, walk or drive to the polling station, stand in line – sometimes for hours – and cast a ballot (mail-in ballots helped alleviate some of that inconvenience in the 2020 US election)?

What motivates Trump supporters is the very problem that needed to be savoured prior to beginning to understand a path towards a possible solution, namely Democratic victory. And the answer, many would argue, is anger or frustration. Survey after survey confirms that Trump's supporters were upset about a lot of things – hence the affinity with a slogan that promised to "make America great again". But it takes something to really incite that voter to the extent of moving the individual from the political *supporter* category to the *active voter turnout* category. More than enough studies have concluded that it appears Hillary Clinton was a key factor in helping achieve that very outcome in 2016. A voter base reacted to Mr. Trump, supporting his approach, his words, and his ideas. That support carried over and "pinged" against an individual, Mrs. Clinton, someone who presumably personified their anger or frustration, thus providing ample motivation to turn out on Election Day.

More than a few political analysts had made the cautionary note that the Democrats would confront political failure if they chose a presidential candidate for the 2020 campaign who was flamboyant, charismatic, and magnetic. Why? Isn't that exactly what an action committee of a political party would be looking for in a candidate? Part of the answer is that Trump supporters were already angry. Someone confronting their anger with panache and charisma could help to motivate them even more, to turn out on Election Day, and possibly give Mr. Trump a second term. A candidate with impeccable qualifications and experience, but who is more middle-of-the-road, non-offensive, like Joe Biden, wouldn't necessarily ignite the flames under Trump supporters – in other words, wouldn't motivate them to vote against a candidate.

Of course, there is a double-edged sword in that sort of strategizing. The risk was that the non-offensive candidate might not even motivate Democratic supporters on Election Day, the only day that makes or breaks the outcome. So, imagine if Democratic central planners masterfully crafted a choice of the first female and first non-white vice-presidential candidate in order to help propel significant Democratic supporters to make the effort and cast a vote. The risk, and there always is one, is that Harris might have incited the very anger that propelled Trump supporters in the first place. But it was a well-executed option, and sufficient numbers of people "bought the product": non-offensive, older and middle-of-the-road balanced with youthfulness, charisma and inclusion. The Democrats savoured their problem. They demonstrated how to "fall in love" with a problem, and only then did they begin crafting a possible solution.

Of course, the complexities that produced the electoral outcomes in 2016 and 2020 were, and are, far greater that the simplification offered here. Our point is to consider and appreciate the challenge that confronts a content creator prior to offering solutions. What message and persona best transmits the objective? So, this discussion of politics simplifies the actors, the processes and the variables involved in order to highlight the importance of correctly knowing a problem prior to embarking on the journey of developing solutions in any given project of promotional outreach.

And yes, an electoral campaign is a "production" entailing narrative, personalities, plot, outreach and the building of a base of consumer infrastructure; it also exemplifies the very essence, the pinnacle, of content creation and promotion.

Our objective in this section, to use an old expression, has been to illustrate the importance of "not putting the cart before the horse". Prior to designing any solutions, and well before selecting methods and techniques, savour your problem, learn to know it and understand it. Once you possess that knowledge, you are in a position to select methods and techniques that reflect the problem, to reach out to your target group with authority, and influence their choices or their actions. The composite of that influence and authority, as we have seen through the example of the Democrats and Joe Biden (which, in reality, also evolved with a healthy degree of good fortune and a myriad other externalities) is power.

3

How do you effectively promote a cause or issue? These things are always important (at least to one person), sometimes intangible, often emotive and compelling, and reside in a universe of other causes and issues that seems never-ending in size and quantity.

War, hunger, food security, poverty, climate change, affordable housing, inclusion, drunk driving, biodiversity, animal shelters, tax fairness, education, clean water. Your alma mater. Your church or place of worship. The local action committee or political party. A community service organization.

There are probably as many causes and issues out there as there are words in a standard dictionary: too many to count. More importantly, there are too many for anyone to really take notice. So how do you raise the volume, get attention, recruit people to your point of view and maintain that momentum?

It's important to state up front what may be obvious to some readers. First, there is no single, cookie-cutter approach. Second, just because what you did worked well before doesn't mean it will again.

Is promotion the same as getting attention? Consider the following: a person standing in the middle of a downtown street, wearing a clown costume and banging pots and pans, will certainly generate attention, and some of that attention will, no doubt, be recycled throughout the day on social or traditional media. The question is how to maintain that attention, and how to translate the awareness into action. What was the intention of getting that attention? Here is where things are not at as easy as they seem.

Let's consider another story. I was recently approached by a fellow who wanted to raise awareness of a disease he has lived with all his life, and one that would ultimately shave at least a few years from his expected lifespan. Who wouldn't be sympathetic? He explained that advances in medical treatments were happening in different parts of the world, and they were showing some signs of success. Those treatments, however, were not available in his country. Not surprisingly, he wanted to access those treatments, and he wanted everyone who also lived with the disease to benefit as well. He was passionate and committed to making sure as many people as possible learned about the disease he was living with, as well as the positive changes that these new treatments could make.

Yet he was a little unclear about why he wanted to do that. While he explained that treatments existed in other countries and should be brought to his, he wasn't altogether clear about his goal.

This is completely normal. Most people don't know what their goal is.

Did he want the public to support the need for medical treatment? If so, the problem was that the public probably didn't know much about the disease to begin with – hence the need for at least some education as a first step (which is a different type of content creation and promotion altogether).

But why bring the public into the equation in the first place, I asked. What if they say, "That disease is horrible. But there are so many other things that need funding"? End of story.

So, let's assume for a moment that money had nothing to do with the outcome. Would the public then sympathize? Perhaps. Let's say they did. So what? How does that sympathy translate into the government updating regulations so that the treatment he heard about could be imported into the country? Should the messaging then be targeted to elected officials, who presumably could influence the process of writing or amending regulations? Or should the effort focus on the government bureaucrats who administer and manage the process? Furthermore, just because there is access doesn't necessarily mean there is affordability. The treatment might be approved for import, but could he or anyone else realistically afford it? A level of subsidy would need to accompany the approval of the treatments to ensure affordability, and this, again, is an entirely different target of promotion.

Through that brief conversation, we identified several goals: public support; political support; policy change; access to the medical treatment; and improved lives.

So, there were at least five goals, with many more objectives, and each of those goals entailing multiple steps. Yet he was hoping that a single solution existed.

Again, his approach in thinking is completely normal. Most people will say something like, "Well, I want to get as many Facebook likes for my petition." They'll explain their thinking, but few will acknowledge the need for these efforts to translate into action - and a clearly defined action, at that.

Someone, somewhere, employed the petition as a form of advocating their cause. While petitions certainly have their appropriate place, this doesn't mean the petition is useful in and of itself, much less a go-to solution. This brings us back to the need to recognize that there isn't a single solution, and just because it worked before shouldn't lead one to believe that it will necessarily work again.

It is also notable that as quickly as something can go viral through a social media platform or series of networks, the demographics of those platforms can also change with surprising speed. The platforms, networks and demographics should not be considered unchanging and secure. The primary user demographics for Facebook in its first few years were considerably different than those from, say, 2019. Those differences are even more augmented because of new and different groups of users being drawn to the platform, sometimes as a result of social or economic change (a pandemic that kept many people at home, for example).

So what worked last year, on a platform that proved effective at that time, won't necessarily deliver the success you hope for when executed this year. The composition and demographics users, as well as user engagement, can shift and alter quite fast.

The point here is to know the platform. Look closely at the user demographics within the geography you hope to mobilize. Which leads us to another important question: why would anyone assume that you can mobilize even one person solely through social media platforms?

Some of the most effective apps embrace the old-fashioned word-of-mouth form of promotion: tell a friend, tell a family member. It's a personal, respected and trustworthy endorsement of the product, service, message or cause.

As a closing thought in this section, I'm reminded of a lecture I once gave to a university class studying promotional outreach and advocacy methods for various political and social causes.

I cautioned these young women and men to not rely exclusively on digital media simply because it's fast, newer or easy. Anyone can sign her or his name to an electronic petition as easily as pressing a button. There is really not much engagement or thought happening in the process. And the problem increasingly is that legislators know this, which is why e-petitions have limited effectiveness. Your Member of Congress or Member of Parliament knows that your electronic petition, despite its volume of digital signatures, has limited authority.

In contrast, two mail bags filled with letters or postcards, let's say, each hand-written and signed, represent considerably more effort, thought and authority. Like the closing court scene in *A Miracle on 34th Street*, when bags and bags of Post Office letters are presented to the judge, carefully choose the most suitable medium to parlay your message. Do it right, and you'll make a lasting impact.

4

Corporate social positioning is a relatively new thing.

Companies typically set out to create something, sell something, or distribute something. It matters little whether the company is a sole proprietorship, a partnership or an incorporated entity. Regardless of the structure, or the product or the service, the company is established to make money. While generating sufficient revenue to cover expenses might constitute the making of money, if a company isn't making a profit, particularly over longer periods of time, the company's existence is limited. A profit is required at some point in the process.

Not so long ago, companies avoided unnecessary risk (at least in the sense that such risk could not be accurately measured). The voices representing the company, the president or the chief executive officer, namely some form of corporate leadership, typically sought to avoid ruffling too many feathers, upsetting too many people. Taking a political position, or social stance, was considered too risky and not consistent with the mission of making money. Why offend some when those people might someday be the very customers you need.

Gradually things have changed. In the 1990s and 2000s, companies wanted to be seen as ecologically responsible, sometimes having extended themselves to emphasize the environmental friendliness of what they produced or sold. Being socially responsible, it turned out, was a good hook to sell more, and make more money. It became so widespread that even those not authentically "environmental" were adopting the stance. For those companies and products, this really was an updated version of the old "new and improved" marketing gimmick.

Then, many companies began to align their sponsorship with social causes. A typical Pride Parade in New York or Toronto is wallpapered with corporate sponsorship. Big banks and insurance companies, traditionally some of the most conservative of corporate entities, spend significant dollars to let people know that they, too, are inclusive and proud (and, to boot, are tapping into a significant market of wallets).

This is not to say that senior executives and corporate leadership isn't or hasn't been genuinely supportive of environmental or social causes. It's simply the case that the alignment of corporate messaging with a cause was considered excessively risky unless a significant demographic base could be delivered.

Things seem to have changed again. Some call it "mission creep", while others criticize the practice as "woke capitalism".

An equally fascinating example looks at the pressure for changing a name and the corporate response to that pressure: the threat by corporate partners to remove their sponsorship of a Washington football team as part of an effort to pressure the team to eliminate its nickname, "Redskins". Even retailers had threatened to pull team merchandise if the nickname remained. In due course, the name was eliminated, and the team played its 2020-21 season without that moniker. Since then, the team has rebranded using a new nickname. Corporate social positioning paved a path toward corporate re-branding and the changing of monikers.

Another team, this time from the world of professional baseball, also with a nickname that many considered as a derogatory expression and an affront to indigenous peoples, announced its plan to remove the moniker and re-brand around the same time. Grassroots objections to the nickname, "Indians", blossomed over many years. And the social tide seemed to land in 2021.

Social pressure effected and re-brand, and Cleveland's baseball team commenced their 2022 season with completely new brand infrastructure and a new nickname, "Guardians".

The trend is also documented in Canada. Here we look to a professional football team in Edmonton, which rebranded from the former nickname, "Eskimos", to the current moniker, "Elks". In this instance, a significant part of the social pressure to change the name originated from a Canadian insurance company that was a prime sponsor of the team. In the Canadian example, the insurance company in question had been a sponsor of the team for several years, according to the press release the company issued at the time.

One might ask why the insurance company's corporate social positioning didn't call for a name change years prior? What suddenly changed? Why was the name Eskimos considered acceptable for many years, only to be viewed with disdain in the early 2020s? Then again, the change occurred, so one might ask: what does it matter?

Some observers refer to such examples as corporate mission creep, others consider these examples as decisive leadership defined by and aligned with prevailing with social values; still, there are critics who consider all this an expression of "woke capitalism" that is harmonized with a tide of "cancel culture".

In one sense, asking why corporate re-branding was necessary shouldn't matter if the "offending" moniker has been eliminated. However, such measure can also appear inauthentic, attempting to demonstrate but lacking in social leadership, and inconsistent with the personality of that corporation, that service or product.

Is it all that bad for the private sector and the business world to adopt social causes and social positioning, even if it rings of me-too-ism? After all, one could say that governments can only do so much, and that the private sector has a legitimate role to play, that it carries authority and influence, and therefore has a certain degree of power in communication. Perhaps.

This recent trend of companies and company leadership having embraced social positions is also a recent topic of discussion by many media outlets. On January 8, 2021, for example, *BloombergBusinessNews.ca* asked its readers the following online poll question: Do you support CEOs who speak out on situations? The question, in this instance, was asked in the context of the chaotic disturbances – and deaths – on Capital Hill in Washington, DC, that occurred days prior. More than 4,000 people took part in the poll. A whopping 68% said YES, that CEOs who speak out on social issues demonstrate social awareness. Fewer than a third of respondents said NO, that the focus of a CEO should be profit. While the poll was informal and certainly not scientific in any way, the results are consistent with the rising trend in corporate social positioning, and the view that private companies should use their authority and influence to promote social causes.

A 2022 analysis by *The Economist* dived deeper into the trend, when, in an article in its "special report" on social corporate goals, stated, "do-goodery has become all the rage." The article continues: "That is most obvious from the embrace of stakeholder capitalism, which redefines corporate success as serving not just shareholders but employees, suppliers and the wider community….[C]ompany bosses have used their commitment to social causes to speak out on issues ranging from racial inclusion to gay rights to climate change." ("Internalising the externalities", Special report on ESG investing, *The Economist*, July 23rd, 2022).

It useful to remain mindful that the ultimate purpose of any company is to make money - and that their very existence must be based on the realization of profit. There are instances during which a social momentum helps provide a fresh perspective on a company's goals, mission, and sometimes even its identity (or branding). This is not only inspirational, but it can represent significant opportunity for the company or organization.

As we have seen with some social causes, as a form of content promotion, the importance of the issue can be fundamental to some, but find only a finicky and temporary appeal among others. Moreover, corporate leadership, unlike political leadership, is both unelected and unaccountable to the public. So, any authority and influence they exert on social causes must be received with a healthy mix of optimism and caution.

5

There so many issues at stake today in launching a new product or service. The majority of start-up businesses fail within the first year. Moreover, traditional bricks-and-mortar businesses (those things that typically composed the main streets in our neighbourhoods and towns) are, at best, living a precarious existence. So, with all these challenges, with so much going against the efforts to advance your product, cause or service, are there any basic principles in which we can still place our confidence?

Sometimes old wisdom seems so sensible that one would think it were as common as air. Yet it is such common sense that we sorely miss in today's world.

So this section shares some reflections in the context of the memoirs of … P.T. Barnum.

Of all people to reference in today's world featured by the increasingly popular sanctimonious blame-game! The man who reputedly disparaged his customers, clients, people in general! Or did he?

P.T. Barnum, generally known as the circus man, and certainly one who strikes a divisive note among many people today, was a masterful promoter and creator of narrative. Regardless of one's opinions or views about circuses, the name, Barnum and Bailey Circus, is widely known, and its origins date back to 1871. That is one heck of a legacy for a company. As for the man, himself, he excelled at nearly everything he engaged in professionally.

One reason contributing to his success is that he knew he was in a business that needed people, namely customers. To need customers, you must know how to reach out to them, speak to them, capture and maintain their attention. Barnum was a master of his craft because he knew people, and, more importantly, he enjoyed getting to know and understand people. Whether we call it a love of people or a dedication to service, the importance of that dotted line between the business and the customer must never diminish. Barnum wrote in his memoirs: "Be polite and kind to your customers. Politeness and civility are the best capital ever invested in business. The truth is, the more kind and liberal a man is, the more generous will be the patronage bestowed upon him."

Picture yourself venturing into a store, whether to browse or to make a specific purchase you already have in mind. Online, sometimes a chat window pops up, welcoming you and any questions you might have, which gives you that human connection as well as the feeling that you are considered both welcome and important. You might experience a similar feeling when you walk into a physical store, a small shop, let's say, and the clerk behind the counter looks up, smiles, and welcomes you, sometimes thanking you for the taking the time to visit and shop.

Yet how many times in your experience, does the sales representative, who is sometimes the owner, ironically, not even bother to look up or say hello?

These are observations on common courtesy; a foundational principle in how to promote, how to conduct outreach, how to connect, and how to sell. It's funny, though, how manners and common courtesy seem less evident today when businesses are flogging their wares. And economic analysts wonder why some businesses go under?

Courtesy cannot guarantee success; but it is the key ingredient in guaranteeing that you know and fully understand the paramount importance of people.

Barnum knew people because he liked getting to know people. He was also an elected official in Connecticut, a position difficult to secure without knowing how to connect with people. He had a keen sense of what it took to get a message across to people, how to make the desired impact.

He intuitively knew that you couldn't recruit people to your cause or sell people a product or service until you had their understanding. In fact, he often said that the object in promotion is to make the public understand what you've got to sell.

Remember our friend, whom we discussed in an earlier section that talked about social causes, that fellow who was used as an example of how most people tend to omit steps in their thinking? The public needed to understand his medical issue, how it impacted his life, why treatments could help and how. They needed the narrative, the content.

So how does one, according to Barnum, work towards making people understand what you're promoting?

a) He cautioned that the reader of a newspaper does not see the first insertion of an ordinary advertisement. That does not constitute a failure, but a simple fact. So, there must be a "second insertion".
b) The second insertion he sees, but does not read.
c) The third insertion he reads.
d) The fourth insertion he looks at the price.

e) The fifth insertion he speaks of it to his wife.

f) The sixth insertion he makes the purchase.

The "insertion" of today could be in the form of a traditional print advertisement in a newspaper or magazine, as it was in Barnum's day. It could be in the form of direct mail, be it a flyer, postcard or unsolicited letter. Today, it could also mean a radio ad, a television commercial, paid message on a news/content channel, an audio spot in a podcast or audio book, any form of content (still image, audio, animated or text) in any one of the online platforms out there (be it a more common-styled website or multi-platform social media feed).

Remember, it took six insertions for a promotion to transform a potential target audience member into an active buyer in Barnum's day. So one shouldn't be surprised that in today's world, featured by masses of multiple forms of messaging in multiple directions simultaneously, one or two paid appearances of your message on Facebook, Twitter or Reddit just isn't going to cut it.

Establishing a presence takes time and perseverance. Making a connection with customer requires courtesy and an authentic interest in people.

6

One of the most unpredictable, one of the trickiest, efforts in promoting your content, is found in knowing which "song" is the "hit". By song, we refer to anything that becomes the hallmark, the signature, the one "thing" that speaks to an audience. It's fascinating how often that "thing" happens unintentionally, somewhat accidently. That "thing" is the visual identifier. The band, Rush, never consciously embarked on using the "starman" image as its "thing". It happened. It became the visual identifier. The United States Senator, Bernie Sanders, probably never sought out to brand himself with hand-knitted mittens. It just kind of worked. Those simple woolen hand-warmers inadvertently became his visual identifier.

A visual identifier is that something that exemplifies your personality, your brand, your image, what you stand for and represent. While it can be a logo, a visual identifier quite often is something else entirely.

As with jurisdictions around the globe, Ontario requires drivers to affix an alpha-numeric identification plate to all moving vehicles. Plates have been issued by the government since the advent of the automobile. Over the decades, the design of the plate has evolved, featuring different colour contrasts during different times. The main image, though, has always been a crown, an image that recalls the heritage of the Province. At times, the crown has been left-justified, while at other times placed bottom-centre. Until recently, that is.

In 2019 the Ontario Government announced that the Province's vehicle plates would be redesigned with new technologies, and the government would begin issuing these to the public in February of 2020. Newer technologies on plate design were being introduced in various jurisdictions. Since there were also quality concerns with the previous batch of the government-issued license plate (under a different governing party and premier), it was deemed an appropriate time to update the design as well as to adopt the new technology.

Preliminary images were released in early 2019. Aside from partisan-tinged commentary, there really weren't any significant public issues with the design of the new plates. The province's colour combination of blue and white was prominent, the updated slogan gave a nod to nostalgia, and the design featured an updated logo of the Ontario government, a stylized trillium.

So, Ontarians were being introduced to an updated brand, an updated logo, and one that this author quite liked. However, no one at that time could have guessed that the plate itself would become a visual identifier of the government as well as its missteps or successes associated with the launch of the plates.

The updated plates were released according to schedule. Brand new plates with brand new designs began replacing plates with old designs and quality issues that had been issued by and associated with a previous governing party. The new plates were becoming a kind of hallmark of a brand new government and what it was all about. That's the good news. The unfortunate part of the story is just how potentially powerful the plates as visual identifiers had become.

The new plates could not be read in the dark, according to officials in local police departments, as well as national border officials. The new product was faulty.

As gnawing as this would have been for officials in the Ontario government, as upsetting as it might be for anyone issuing a new product accompanied by a re-brand, mistakes happen. But in this instance, the mistake had the power to become a visual identifier.

What is the purpose of a vehicle plate, a licence plate on your car or truck?

The plate is part of system of identifying the ownership and registration of a vehicle. It certifies legally that the vehicle is road-worthy and otherwise not questionable, and this information is linked to registries in insurance companies, police and government databases, and border systems.

Without this system, we would have uncertainty and chaos surrounding car ownership, accidents, liability, sale and purchase of vehicles, to name a few issues. So it is evidentiary. It is proof. It is a tool that contains sets of data and information.

What else is a vehicle plate? It's a little piece of advertising, sometimes displaying your name, company or favourite cause, which, by the way, can also serve as a source of revenue for the government.

Is it anything else? It says to people, especially when we're driving outside our jurisdictions, "hey, look where I'm from". So imagery associated with your home, a famous landmark, say, will be used to "shout-out" about your country, province, territory or state. Perhaps one of the most effective shout-outs in plate design and imagery comes from Canada's Northwest Territories. Heck, the entire plate is cut into the shape of a polar bear.

So, circling back, we revisit the purpose of the new plates: improvement and visual rebranding. The product failed in the first category. One can reference the evaluations and feedback from police, who claimed that they could not read the plates at night, as well as those responsible for radar and photo systems, and from border security. A total recall and replacement announcement confirms the level of failure.

But there is another failure – or, rather, *potential* failure – specifically in the second category of visual rebranding. The failure can also be seen from a branding and promotional perspective because the power of the visual identifier was so strong.

Visual identifiers can help propel a narrative or company or government, but those very identifiers can serve as constant reminders of failure. Herein is the most serious risk in not knowing the power of an exemplar of your company as a visual identifier. The product itself - something attached to the front and rear of moving vehicles - is visual, easily identifiable, one that has action, personality and image all sewn together into one crystalizing moniker. Moreover, the vehicle plate is, as a brand, a moving advertisement. Wherever that vehicle travels, whenever someone sees that image, the misstep or success is reinforced.

Sometimes, missteps can be overcome by time, context and externalities. In this case, the functional failure of the plate, coupled with its power as a visual identifier, tended not to resonate publically, as the issue took backseat to a global health pandemic and its associated social and economic measures. Fortune prevailed, and this part of the failure in branding was only potential, something that almost happened.

That said, the lesson is this: when planning a re-brand or a new narrative, you also have to factor in possible failure and what the ramifications and costs might be. When the risks of success or failure can be branded, and serve as a visual identifier, the questions associated with "What if we tried to …?" become as important as the appeal of the imagery or the quality of the narrative. Plan your actions as harmoniously as you can.

7

Brands and logos are usually thought of by many people as visual functions of content creation and promotion. This is not surprisingly since these things typically do manifest in something visual. Did you know that audible tools can promote a product, service of cause, and sometimes with greater effect? Think of the commercial jingle, an audible promotional tool you've likely heard countless numbers of times. But music has far greater potential and a deeper history in promotion than through the use of commercial jingles and melodies.

Among all the things that music can represent to a listener, music is also an important tool in promotion. Music has been used to woo crowds for centuries. From parades, church hymns, and circuses, to street organ grinders and commercial jingles, music captures attention, it helps cultivate appeal, community and affinity, and it ultimately contributes to selling, recruiting or retaining, as the case may be.

Music has been used in product promotion for about as long as anyone's memory serves.

Much has been written about this, so there's little need to explore that application of music as a promotional tool in this book. However, there are many other promotional applications of music.

The use of music as a promotional tool in politics and related political messaging is particularly interesting.

Without question, Americans have mastered this medium, and still serve as a benchmark. An American election is as much a pageant as it is an exercise in democracy. It's so effective that people want to be part of it. The US President even has an unofficial anthem, "Hail to the Chief".

A considerable quantity of messaging has found its voice in music: "Yankee Doodle Dandee", "Give Peace a Chance", "Sunday Bloody Sunday", "A Change is Gonna Come", "Ohio". The songs themselves often transcend their intended meanings, and have become embedded as popular pieces of music. Yet, these are just as political as the anthems played at a White House celebration.

The use of live musical performance has also been commandeered to raise awareness and help change policy. This process, advocacy, is another form of content creation and promotion.

Farm Aid in the United States was started by Willie Nelson, Neil Young and John Mellencamp in 1985 to raise awareness about the loss of family farms, and to raise funds to help keep families in locally based, family-owned and - operated agriculture. Concert festivals were used to lure the crowds, transmit the message, and generate donations.

In Toronto, in the early 2000s, when the city was listed on the steer-clear-of list by the World Health Organization due to a respiratory virus, the SARS outbreak, the use of live music, and its accompanying crowds of fans with money to spend, was corralled to help create a different narrative about health safety in the city. And it turned out that performances by the Rolling Stones, AC/DC and Rush (plus another 20 or so performers) was an effective salve against the economic downturn associated with SARS. Nearly half a million people attended, helping generate massive media coverage the world over.

Music was used to help change the narrative, to create new content, and to promote that messaging.

Another interesting use of music in a political format was recently found right inside the United Nations headquarters in New York City. This was seen through lobbying efforts, another art of content creation, persuasion and promotion.

As a brief aside, lobbying, simply put, refers to the promotion of a message, aimed directly at government or elected officials, with the intent of introducing or changing a policy, program or law. The term, lobbying, by the way, originates in the British parliamentary tradition, and was used to describe the practice of conducting conversations with members of parliament, particularly cabinet ministers, which at one time took place in the "lobby" of the entrance to the House of Commons.

While lobbying takes a different form in the UN, it is lobbying, nonetheless. Every now and then, elections are held for membership on one of the dozens of committees in the UN architecture. Delegates representing countries and non-governmental organizations (NGOs) appeal to other delegates attempting to persuade their votes. Frequently these appeals to colleagues include incentives ranging from special events that offer cultural cuisines, to educational materials, posters, trinkets and souvenirs, and - yes, music. These appeals usually have some effect. Who wouldn't want to take in a live musical performance with some hors d'oeuvres and cocktails and the end of a long day of deliberations in a UN meeting hall?

In a 2020 bid for membership of the Security Council, several countries were vying for the coveted and prestigious seat. Tastes and samples of various products from each contending country were offered to those considering the candidates. Most relevant to this discussion, based on a mix of fact and rumour, tickets to musical performances by artists of each country's delegates were distributed to voting members.

The Irish wooed their colleagues with U2 tickets, while the Canadians tapped into the power of Celine Dion. It was thought by many in that round of voting that Canada would surely secure a seat (not solely because of the tickets, of course). Alas, as it turns out, tickets to a Celine Dion performance weren't enough of a draw for voting delegates. Ireland, on the other hand, pushed its candidacy for the Security Council seat with overtures that involved free tickets to Riverdance and a U2 performance. Ireland ultimately won over the votes.

Did the choice of musicians affect the outcome of voting delegates' decisions in any real way? Not likely. One would venture to guess that delegates would have been captivated by a performance by either of these musical powerhouses, and that more substantive policy issues would have steered the voting outcome.

One thing is certain: your selection of music that is intended to get your point across must also appeal to those making the ultimate decision.

Music can be a powerful tool to catch attention and win over a potential customer or vote. It has the power to embody the message you want to promote. Music can be one of your most effective transmitters. Music has also the potential of outlasting your campaign, regardless of whether that campaign was tailored for an election, a new product launch, or securing enough votes to win a seat on the UN Security Council.

The traditional "jingle" was typically a short, original composition designed to highlight key words and, most importantly, grab a potential customer's ears in a catchy way. This is the type of promotional tool that many people are most accustomed to hearing. Other musical pieces will borrow and rearrange an already composed and published piece, usually one that was popular at the time, and use the rearranged version for the promotion. This method is a little riskier, in that the marketing teams responsible for the campaign typically try to tap into the "cool" factor of the song or the artist; however, they had better have some first-hand, experiential knowledge about that artist or song. Of course, a negative outcome of a piece of music is that it utterly turns off an entire segment of the population.

While the benefits can be monumental, the risks always exist for any piece of music. Music is emotive, and those emotions and context associations of music can easily go either way.

Repetition and perseverance also play a factor when considering the choice or form of music. It's one thing to recruit a band to play a one-off performance to raise awareness of a cause, but altogether quite a different matter for an ad campaign in high rotation on radio or television that uses a rendition of a previously popular song.

Like anything that is potentially powerful, approach the use of music as a promotional tool with understanding and healthy caution. Know why you want to use music in your messaging. What do you hope to achieve with it? Is it the most suitable promotional tool for your content, message and campaign?

8

In the previous section we discussed music applications in the art of content creation and promotion. This section will consider the use of something related, but quite distinct and even shorter in composition than a commercial jingle or anthem: the soundmark and the audio logo.

An audio logo is a tool that is actually a sound trademark. Sound is used to perform the trademark function of uniquely identifying the commercial original of products or services. They are known by several names: audio logo, sound trademark, soundmark, and probably a few more. So, what exactly are these things?

You're probably more intimately familiar with these tools that you might think.

Imagine yourself in a movie theatre sometime in the 1980s or 1990s (if you're old enough). The coming attractions were over. Commercial ads had played. The film was about to being - but first, viewers experienced something else: a soundmark.

The THX soundmark was first introduced in the early 1980s. The sound was used on trailers and played in THX-certified movie theatres. It was used to let the audiences in movie theatres know that the film they were about to see used THX technology, that the theatre was equipped to give the audience a full THX-quality sound experience. There was no catchy music, no words in the piece. The total audio running time was less than 20 seconds. It was a sound wave that built to a crescendo, then faded out. It was produced and owned by Lucasfilm.

Over time, viewers anticipated that part of the experience. The soundmark became associated with the beginning of a film. The sound itself was cool to experience as it swelled to that cinema-filling rush, engaging the full realm of the audio system. It inadvertently also let latecomers know that the film was beginning.

That soundmark is one of the audio trademarks with a longer running time. Whether they ran for two seconds or twenty seconds, they did much same as a visual logo - performing the function of uniquely identifying the product or service.

There are many more examples, and some go back decades.

Take the 20th Century soundmark. Even if we might not correctly identify which studio owns it, we instantly recognize the drum arrangement as identifying a movie studio. For generations of film buffs, the 20th Century audio logo has introduced the company's product and reinforced its brand through an assortment of complementary media.

The sound logo is one of the tools of sound branding, along with the commercial jingle, brand music, and brand theme. We hear them as a distinct sequence of sound.

One of the earlier examples of this type of branding was used by NBC in the United States. The NBC "three chimes" served as a form of network identification. Television viewers knew that once those chimes sounded, something promising, something entertaining, and presumably trustworthy (since its broadcast license had been granted by government), was about to begin play in their living rooms.

More recently, Home Box Office, or HBO, has used its soundmark prior to the beginning of every episode of each show it has produced and broadcast or streamed.

The Netflix audio trademark falls into a similar category. Again, we hear that sound at the beginning of every Netflix show we watch. Not only is it the acoustic equivalent of a visual logo, it complements the animation of the logo, thereby doubly reinforcing the recognition of the brand, and taking content creation and promotion to even more refined levels.

Soundmarks have also blossomed in the realm of consumer goods.

Intel computer chips uses a very simple, four- note soundmark with a total running time of less than a couple of seconds. This classic soundmark by Intel signalled to consumers that the computer they were considering was built with Intel chips. You only needed to hear the sound, and you knew what it was. Its simplicity makes it a very powerful example of audio branding.

Another example of audio branding in consumer products is seen in the mobile phone. Telephone advances in the 1990s and 2000s developed at an incredibly fast pace. Differentiation is critical to success for any company and product. One of the early leaders, Nokia, chose to distinguish itself through its soundmark ringtone. This ringtone is one of the longer compositions in audio branding, but has become classic and, in some ways, has taken on a life of its own. Not only has the short melody been used as a promotional tool in television commercials, but it was the default ringtone for the phones themselves, reinforcing the brand on the screen, on the radio, and through the telephone handset, lending itself to a very different user experience.

Unlike a jingle or melody, intellectual property protection for soundmarks and audio logos is still comparatively new, with much discussion and debate continuing around questions such as, "Can Company B put a trademark on a simple sound, or a single note or two?" It was only in 2012 that the MGM lion's roar was given support by the US Federal Court. Interestingly, in that same year, the Canadian Trademarks Office allowed for the registration of soundmarks. Even today, while soundmarks are registrable, and soundmarks can receive protection in law, the process is still less than cut-

and-dried than is the case for more traditional trademarks and copyrights.

During the advent of the commercial Internet, the world wide web, in the 1990s, some early versions of websites featured soundmarks in an opening page. And as promotion becomes more digital, audio branding becomes more important. You'll want something to distinguish and identify your podcast, your website or blog, your YouTube channel. It can become a key part of the personality, and a very powerful identifier with the potential for multiple uses.

As with many things in life, simple can often be better. Yet, while it might sound odd, creating a four-note sound logo can sometimes be even more challenging that a four-line, 30-second musical jingle.

So next time you're listening to the radio, or watching a commercial, movie or TV show, see if you know the brand just by hearing the soundmark. Try to become aware of these tools when visiting websites or listening to podcasts. Think about what that sound tells you about the company's content, and what it is trying to promote.

9

Online shopping has exploded in volume and popularity, especially at an accelerated pace since early 2019; and so, too, have the opportunities associated with innovation. New products and promotional tools can certainly be innovative. A more exciting breed of innovation, though, is when we see a convergence of worlds, an integration of the digital realms, a form of social commerce or e-integration.

Put simply, social commerce happens when someone sells something directly on social media. The entire experience, from locating what the customer wants, to comparison shopping, purchase, check-out and letting others know about your choice, all takes place on one platform. This is the integration that makes social commerce truly innovative.

E-commerce, on the other hand, has been around much longer. This occurs when, say, a store puts its catalogue of products on a website or app. The customer visits that specific location, selects, purchases, and checks-out. The customer closes the app or leaves the website.

Social commerce places the customer at the centre of everything, and there is no need for the customer or user to leave. In contrast, e-commerce offers a technology or service online, allows the customer to visit, but, most importantly, like a bricks-and-mortar store, provides no further incentive or reason to remain in that location once the transaction is complete. Social commerce is a more fulsome, more robust, form of e-integration.

YouTube, TikTok, Snapchat and Instagram lead the pack in social commerce. You probably guessed that Millennials and Generation Z constitute the majority of users. Video is the primary form of content, and short, snappy clips, at that. Then, through the video content, social media users are connected directly to a brand by simply touching the screen. The best feature of social commerce? The fact that everything is built around mobility: it operates across multiple platforms in an integrated way, and it's tailored to the mobile device. E-commerce means offering a product or service online, quite often through what started as a website and later became transposed onto a dedicated app. E-commerce lacks the social media experience, whereas social commerce blends e-commerce with social media experiences.

An enthusiast of digital innovation would rightly be fascinated with this growing trend. In Western markets, social commerce is trending towards big bucks. Yet, that same enthusiast would be doubly fascinated to see the trends as they have developed in China. While we're moving closer to e-integration in the West, the convergence of the realms that give rise to social commerce are really still in their infancy, and have not yet transcended generational boundaries in a substantive way.

China features a fascinating integration of live streaming, content creation, promotion, retail, person-to-person communication, and banking. In this integrated mix, the consumer is central, where all else radiates from that consumer- centric position.

In contrast, western economies, while featuring astounding forms of innovation, still have "silos" that haven't yet broken down. Finance is a silo separate from content streaming, and both are separate (though at times can be coordinated) from retail. In the West, innovation is driven by technology, which is a very top-down approach.

The result of the continued existence of silos implies distinct efforts of content creation and promotion.

The market is more highly concentrated in China than in many other places. As well, one finds a significantly higher percentage of mobile users in China (98% of internet users connect through mobile!). While the computer, the processing chip and the world wide web ushered in massive changes in the West, it was the introduction of the integrated mobile device - the gadget that combines the features of a telephone, a device for shopping, ordering, paying, sending condensed messages, taking photos and watching movies - that began making the most profound changes. Ask any official at the United States Postal Service or Canada Post why their revenues had plunged so severely during the 2010s. The mobile device really did change everything, and its mobility and technology opened a new landscape.

China did not evolve as the West did from a base of consumerism. In the West, while there was a sort of convergence of technologies, there were primarily physical in nature (for example, the use of cars and their relationship to getting customers to shopping malls). This is all bricks-and-mortar. As a testament to this fact, today, according to data from various consulting houses, more than 300 million people in the United States have 30 times as many malls as China does - a country with roughly 1.4 billion people.

There's still plenty of physical shopping in China, but the high proliferation of mobile technology, as well as greater economies of scale and intense urbanization that create cheaper delivery options, add another level of attractiveness for Chinese consumers.

The Chinese consumer culture started at a different time and from a different place. That culture has grown in tandem with the proliferation of technology. Social networks and shopping blended together to a far greater and more effective degree than anywhere else. The Chinese consumer culture has evolved with technology, with the consumer positioned as a central figure. Everything else radiates from that point.

The outcome treats content creation and promotion as an integrated process. The vendor relies on the social network of family and friends, who can vouch for the quality and efficacy of the product. Social influencers are integrated as key pitch people, of a sort. The buyer of the product is encouraged to stream reviews and demonstrations, even short dramatic skits. As long as a mobile device is at the ready, and in China those devices reach 98% of the population, the integration works equally well for the remote farmer as it does for an urban jewelry maker. Content creation and promotion are integrated through every part of the system.

This direction in social commerce engages consumers in ways previously unexplored in the West. Some of this is due to Western regulation, which maintains the separation of silos (there is certainly no shortage of anti-trust actions); and some is the result of higher relative prices in the West. Western consumers have a different economic culture. Creating content about the product you purchased, and promoting that content through multiple ways and formats, comes as second nature to many consumers in China. In contrast, far fewer consumers in Western countries hold as much confidence in sharing purchase patterns and spending habits with those who inhabit the digital world. For now, this behaviour is concentrated among the youngest generations (although, the very groups with tremendous buying power).

The harmony of digital and e-integration in China helped create its foundational ascendancy of social commerce. There is some evidence that shows similar trends, though to limited degrees, in a number of African countries as well as those of the Middle East. In these markets (many of which have been categorized as "emerging" or "developing"), research is showing that the "trust factor" is more important. Social commerce may well become a dominant model in these markets as well, but those forces that instill and reinforce confidence and trust appear to be particularly important.

Will we see social commerce develop to a degree as robust as in China? For that to happen, change would be required in many fronts: regulation; consumer behaviour; the number of firms, etc. We have seen convergence of industries and sectors in Western economies: banking and securities brokerage; finance and real estate; retail and credit; and some consumer products with communications (the voice-activated home assistant, for example). But the silos that exist in the West are still considerable. Alternatively, could China see a dampening of the appeal and popularity of social commerce? Is this "thing" still so new that its novelty might diminish with the aging of their society?

Rapid advances in technology can at times be accompanied by surprisingly rapid changes in social or consumer behaviour (the effects of the recent global pandemic on work, school and shopping suggest that some social and consumer behaviour can adapt remarkably fast).

The younger generations in the West may help usher in changes previously unseen that could eventuate towards, or resemble, e-integration and social commerce. These are the consumers who have grown up with, and are situated at the centre of, technology. It is they who seem to have a more intuitive, more integrated approach to shopping, banking, voting, streaming - and content creation and promotion.

10

We just touched on how the "trust factor" plays a bigger role in the development of social commerce in some markets compared to others. For example, while the influencer is central to the effectiveness of social commerce, a user's trust in the authority of that influencer can determine how and to what degree a market of social commerce will develop. Which brings us to the question: why do people believe what is told to them? Why do they trust the content of the message and the source of the promotion?

Let's revisit the earlier section where we considered some of the experience of P.T. Barnum. Although far from fact, popular legend has it that Barnum immortalized the phrase, "There's a sucker born every minute". If that's the case, why would anyone trust his advice, much less dedicate a few pages of a book to discussing it? Herein is a great example of trust and authority. How does anyone know for certain that Barnum ever spoke those words? Whose authority that tells us that he disparaged the customer to such a crass extent gives this legend so much credibility? Interestingly, one should note that while popularly attributed to Barnum, there is no actual evidence that he spoke those words. On the contrary, Barnum was an individual who elevated, not disparaged, the status of his customer. Yet someone at some time has led most people to believe that Barnum was the man who spoke and immortalized the phrase. Why did people believe it to be true? On whose authority?

We have an innate quality of recognizing, perhaps even wanting to recognize, authority of others: "It must be true if was printed in the newspaper."; "They reported it on the evening news."; "It was published on a website." Even the social media platform, Reddit, seems to acknowledge the implicit trust people have in the authority of others: "Where did you hear that," asks one person to another. "I *reddit* somewhere." Clever.

Revisiting Barnum's steps in the promotion of content, we see that the reader (or the listener, or customer, as the case may be), really has nothing at stake until the point of purchase, or the decision to consider a purchase. Prior to that point, the message or narrative is one of informal authority. When the purchase is made, we leap to recognizing the source as formal.

There is still the tendency among people, it seems, to want to recognize the authority in others, be informal or formal. The only difference with the recognition of formal is that the reader, listener or customer becomes active in the process, specifically that a transaction, in some form, occurs. The transaction has a value, and it takes formal authority for someone to hold that level of trust.

When someone has the authority of voice and can measure a level of influence (for example, by the transaction), we then have what some would refer to as power.

The notions of trust, authority and influence in the efforts of content creation and promotion have virtually unlimited potential. So compelling is the potential that the schemer and fraudster have attempted to secure his or her position in the market. Knowing that people want to recognize authority, we have a field wide open for tricksters, profiteers, scammers and the like. They have taken many forms and have occupied virtually every field and profession, twisting the art of content creation and promotion, abusing trust and authority, to their advantage.

In 1962, a "technical expert" informed television viewers in Sweden, who were watching their country's only TV channel, how to "convert" the image on their TV screens into colour. He explained that a simple nylon stocking could be stretched across the black-and-white screen, which would bend light in a way to create the effect of colour. Viewers might then need to "adjust" the effect, by simply moving their heads to the left or to the right. Thousands of viewers, it was later reported, were frantically searching their homes for extra pairs of nylon stockings to stretch over their TV sets. While the entire episode was later attributed to an April Fool's joke, the content and the way it was promoted tapped into people's innate quality of recognizing the authority of others. "It was on the evening news, and an expert explained the process." Ergo, it must true.

Years prior, the radio broadcast of *War of the Worlds*, narrated by Orson Welles, was sent live across the United States. The radio program was aired as fiction, a radio drama, and listeners who heard the program in its entirety were aware of that fact. However, for the thousands who tuned in mid-program, the content sounded more like a news report. The producers never intended to trick anyone. Alas, more than a few reports of suicide were made that evening and the following day, as some listeners could not bear the thought of aliens from another world landing in towns and attacking their civilizations. The authority of the broadcast, and the measured influence it had, culminated in a form of power that few could ever have predicted.

There are many more examples of friendly pranks and unintended hoaxes, some with unintended consequences. Then there are the intended abuses that many of us have experienced or know about: everything from spam emails to "boiler room" telemarketers. Many of these operations target specific demographic groups, such as older seniors, people with language barriers, and low-income households. Yet other target groups can be none of the above. The film, *Boiler Room*, provides an expose of shady brokers and traders of various financial investments. Their targets are professionals who have a bit of surplus cash. These targets, medical doctors and dentists, are convinced - over the phone, by a voice belong to a person whom they had never met - to put their money in investments that turn out to be bogus. The film is a great example of how trust and authority can be abused in the creation and promotion of content. *Matchstick Men* is another in which telemarketers convince people that they had won a "grand prize". All that was needed to claim the prize was the transfer of funds to the telemarketers. The amount, call recipients were told, was roughly equal to the taxes that would be due on such winnings. In this film, people's bank accounts are emptied, prizes were, of course, non-existent or a flaccid version of what was explained to the "prize winner", and the operation regularly closed shop and resumed under a new name, in a new location. It sounded real, people wanted to believe and to trust, and the confidence men who ran the scheme abused the power of how to bend perception, how to promote the content to accentuate what the target wanted to hear, and how to "get out of Dodge" with their pockets full.

One of the more recent types of fraud that play on the authority of content and promotion are the tax collection calls that many Americans and Canadians receive. The caller will tell the "target", that person who answers the phone, that significant income taxes are owed. The caller would then cite multiple, obscure and always false names, regulations and laws from that country's tax authority. Imagine receiving a call from your tax authority: it's likely going to make you feel uncomfortable, worried perhaps. In this scam, callers are told that if they pay even a fraction of the alleged amount owing, through a direct transfer or the opening of access to their bank accounts, that all matters against them would be dropped. Ultimately, thousands of people, and many thousands of dollars, have been the subject of this kind of fraud - the kind that abuses people's innate quality of recognizing the authority of someone or the medium in which the message is transmitted.

Regulatory oversight and the imposition of punitive measures help address some of these concerns. Furthermore, the advent of "fake news" has prompted more than a few decision makers at social media companies to dedicate resources to identifying and removing such content from their platforms.

However, as long as there is opportunity to do something that generates an economic gain, a corresponding percentage of people will identify that opportunity as a potential to scam, scheme and abuse.

Content creation and promotion is, to a degree, part illusion and entails the bending of perception. That said, isn't that act of bending perception really just an abuse of authority and people's trust?

The key take-away here highlights both the opportunity of making an impact with our content and promotional efforts, as well as the responsibility we have to ensure accuracy and integrity, and to identify and avoid any unintended outcomes.

If your product is "new and improved", let people know how exactly it differs from the previous version. If you are offering free access to your online services, don't hide the clause that informs customers of monthly charges that will later appear should explicit cancellation not occur (negative billing). In short, don't get carried away with accentuating something and, in the process, creating and telling a non-truth. Your most important resource - your potential customer, reader, listener, audience member or voter - is the keystone of your efforts, be it to personify your blog, recruit people to a social or political cause, or attempt to reinforce your corporate identify and presence in the broader social realm. While technology is a prime mover in developing the innovation and opportunities of markets, trust is the eternal enabler.

11

A potential customer must be informed about your product or service. This involves a variety of communications and techniques. Whatever your mix, your efforts ultimately help inform a customer whether or not to buy, as well as which supplier is best at that time.

A producer of the best product available won't be generating very much business if no one knows the product exists. In other words, don't run off and build "it" believing that by its very existence your customers will flow. It is often said that the balanced mix of your efforts should be 20% on content creation and 80% on promotion. But promotion must be more than the passing of information. It must be persuasive and it must differentiate. It matters little whether you are launching a new jewelry business online, constructing an election campaign for a political candidate, or advocating for a change in an existing law or regulation, you must be persuasive and you must differentiate.

The fact is, when persuasively promoting, you need the right mix of techniques. Earlier we highlighted the importance of tailoring your mix to your product and target audience at a particular time. In other words, to reiterate, don't replicate past mixes simply because they worked well before - ensure that they do again! Also, you must be in the "long game"; that is to say, to understand and appreciate that your efforts - as Barnum said a century ago - are cumulative, so much so that such efforts may even seem routine. Persistence and perseverance are never old-fashioned.

When starting your considerations of persuasion, sometimes it is more useful to first consider the negatives. What are the disadvantages of the methods of promotion that you are considering? Is there a reason you feel that a particular tactic is more suitable to the target group you're looking at? Can one tactic be measured with greater accuracy than another?

What are the important differences for you when considering between a low-budget or no-budget tactic compared to a full suite of techniques. Can you not afford to provide a free sample, trial or membership?

So, as you might have guessed, persuasion is only one part of the picture; closing the sale is equally important, as this outcome is the all-important measure of success.

Many people claim to be uncomfortable with the notion of "sales". The fact is, like the art of illusion, we are all engaged in sales, whether we know it or not. The art of persuasion is only as useful as the end result: action, agreement, buy-in or a sale. We sell ideas, proposals, our resumes, even our online dating profiles. We try to persuade; we aim to seal the deal or get the buy-in. The buyer is simply the manifestation, the persona, of the outcome we hope to achieve. The buyer can be a potential customer, the potential employer, the voter, your child or spouse, a romantic interest or date.

The effectiveness of your persuasion directly results in the degree to which your desired outcome is achieved.

When considering the tools of persuasion, the use of in-person tactics should never diminish in importance. Buying a new home represents a huge item of consequence in one's life. Nothing can replace the in-person connection that a real estate agent brings to the experience. In fact, that's a big reason why realtors include their faces on their promotional materials (also reinforcing brand, and solidifying confidence and trust). Another arena where the importance of in-person contact is paramount is in election campaigns and voter engagement. A town-hall meeting or door-to-door canvass establishes and reinforces the personal connection that speaks to issues of trustworthiness and confidence. No amount on online or virtual interaction can replace this key piece.

That said, let's consider the digital world and how various online properties can advance or hinder your cause.

Never underestimate your existing contact list. That list is much bigger than most people assume. An old rule-of-thumb once used for assessing the potential effectiveness of insurance associates was to see if the candidate for the job could list 100 contacts - because each of those contacts is a lead. One hundred contacts? Who has that? Well, most of us have at least that. All names likely are not consolidated in one list. The volume increases as soon as you consider the networks you may not even think about: people who attended school, college or university with you; people from a sports team, drama club, musical band or hobby group; people in your neighbourhood; people at your present job as well as past places of work; people in your professional associations or church groups; your medical doctor, your dentist, your lawyer; your local elected officials; your mail carrier; your family members and their family members. This list goes on. And very quickly you will realize that your list is much, much bigger than you once thought. The list expands again for those people who are active on social media, when considering every contact, friend and follower. Starting a base with your own contact list is hugely important.

For many online efforts it is useful to start backwards by first looking at what you hope to achieve. First consider who you want to reach (and don't say "everyone"). Do you want media coverage? Asking end-of-game questions like these helps tailor your content to the medium and the types of people who frequent those platforms or networks.

A legal service provider will have a different audience than someone promoting environmental issues, and a retailer of pick-up trucks will likely be dealing with different issues than the owner of a bicycle shop. A candidate for elected office will want to differentiate between those online groups who chat, debate and criticize from those who are active and are actually eligible and inclined to vote. Someone seeking to raise membership in their church or club would be wasting a monumental amount of time by focusing primarily on existing membership. Your content will vary depending on the path you take.

Make it go viral, some will say. Ok, so what does that mean? Many people tend to embrace the lingo without really knowing what the words mean or how to achieve the result. Viral, online, simply refers to the re-propagation of content. It certainly helps things if that content is sensational in quality or features images that must be "shared". Make no mistake: getting something to go "viral" isn't about having content in the can, so to speak, then making it so. It doesn't happen on its own, despite how important you feel your content may be.

12

Ongoing self-reflection is critical in content creation and promotion. We have to pause occasionally, and ask ourselves, "how do we know we're moving the right direction, especially when so many things around us are moving?" The world today is moving faster than it ever has.

The Shifting Economy

We've been observing, and to an extent experiencing, a shift for quite some time. The ubiquity of mobile devices and the explosion of e-commerce are not only hallmarks of the shift, but they helped usher in newer convergences. It

81

is these convergences that represent the biggest shift in our economic surroundings. The steady decline of traditional bricks-and-mortar retail over the past several years is a symptom. It often takes a "disruptor" to enter the picture and really "blow things up"; that disruptor has been the global coronavirus pandemic (which began to make its impact felt in late 2019). Stay-at-home orders, shutdowns and lockdowns opened the aperture of a wide social acceptance of relying heavily in mobile devices and e-commerce, to such an extent that the shift manifests in widespread closures of entire chains of previously thriving retail empires. Some physical retail will remain and thrive. However, while one might point to the shutdowns as the biggest cause of the decline in physical retail, the trend of retraction was evident prior to the pandemic, and the trend of widespread closures of physical retail will not likely reverse in the foreseeable future. What types of retail our economy shifts towards is still in question.

The Growth of Social Commerce

Convergence is the key word of our times. The more we see the convergence of social media and e-commerce, the greater will be the opportunity for social commerce. We're seeing this convergence to a degree. Yet, as discussed in earlier sections, a market like China's is fundamentally better suited for this type of trend. That said, few could have predicted the degree of disruption caused by the global pandemic. That disruptor could yet help motivate a further breaking down of the silos that characterize Western markets, thereby helping to usher in greater convergences of the elements that create social commerce.

The Ascendancy of Digital Currency

Crypto currency, like Bitcoin, challenges the paradigms of traditional money and banking because of its ability to circumvent such systems. Crypto currency relies on technology instead of the authority of the state that banks rely on. According to Wikipedia: "A cryptocurrency is a digital asset designed to work as a medium of exchange wherein individual coin ownership records are stored in a ledger existing in a form of a computerized database using strong cryptography to secure transactions...typically a blockchain that serves as a public financial transaction database." We are also seeing the early signs of digital versions of paper money currency, traditionally controlled and issued by central banks. The disrupting factor, the pandemic, has served to accelerate the consideration of issuing an official digital currency in many countries. Regardless of when digital and crypto currencies become the norm, we are at a point today where hard-copy money (paper money) has likely reached its summit.

The Impact of Social Media

Earlier we discussed the impact of social media on a company's brand. The influence is undeniable. We also see social media's impact on our traditional sources of news. Giving rise to "fake news", social media has slowly become the predominant source of news and current affairs information for many people. Anyone today can be a reporter, broadcaster or current affairs columnist (each of which contribute significant to the formation of public opinion). While traditional news organizations typically had fact-checkers and proof-readers, today's growing spectrum of social media news rarely has any of these "checks and balances" previously considered a hallmark of quality and trust in traditional news organizations. Another impact is found in revenue loss: traditional news organizations have lost significant revenue to social media sources of news and information - to such an extent that many traditional providers of news in several countries have worked in coalition to change the rules of their own countries to favour their interests and markets. The authority and influence of social media on news, markets and current affairs is also measurable and increasingly profound. For example, the impact of Reddit users on the stock market and stock valuations in February 2021 illustrates the authority and influence of social media; it also highlights how some of today's regulatory systems (vis-à-vis day-trading, in this case) are sometime antiquated. These changes will continue.

The Internet of Things

Convergence is accelerating even on the home front, in our personal lives. AI-driven voice-activated assistants are common devices in homes today. These provide not just answers to questions we might have about the price of gas at the nearest service station or the price of roundtrip airfare; they can provide the news of your choice, weather updates and personal calendar reminders. They can control a wide range of functions, from your audio and video libraries, to shopping, home appliances and security systems, even placing voice calls or composing and sending text messages. And these systems are not limited to the home. AI systems, many of which are voice-activated, are now basic features in just about every automobile. Regular service appointments for your car are as much about updating the operating systems as they are about servicing the physical components of the vehicle.

The volume of change around us can be as exciting as it is dizzying. So how do we know we're moving in the right direction, making our desired impact, with the creation of our content and promotional efforts? Are we really making any difference?

Despite the changes we're experiencing, and will continue to do so for several years to come, the principles that underpin our work never diminish – principles such as establishing a presence, differentiating what you have to offer, relating to your intended group through personality and narrative, and remembering the importance of persistence and perseverance.

One of the greatest benefits of the increasing proliferation of digital systems is data. We're able to measure and monitor metrics and analytics as never before. What's more, much of this data is instantaneous and self-driven at any given time of the day or night.

With that readily available probity of numbers, there might come a time when you see an impact or a measure that you didn't expect. Your cause might have recruited more seniors than ever expected, for example. Your product video might be viewed more frequently in a part of the world that you never considered. This is opportunity. So grab it. Shift the focus and respond accordingly.

What about negative feedback? Someone famously once declared that there is no such thing as bad publicity. The point here focuses on "making what you can with what you have at your disposal".

Several years ago, prior to social media and related apps, a local, relatively pricey restaurant received a scathing review by a well-known food and restaurant critic, and one that was published as a full-page column in a national newspaper. The owner was devastated. He had only been open a couple of months, invested much of his life savings, and worked daily on the floor, greeting customers and overseeing operations. He didn't know what to do. Instead of shying away from what he considered bad publicity, he was advised to embrace it. How? Reprint the review from the newspaper, enlarge it to the size of a poster, and hang it in the front window of the store where passers-by could read it. He couldn't change the fact that the review had been published. So, he embraced its perceived negative publicity, and used it to help change the narrative. Passers-by became curious about this relatively new restaurant that was promoting itself with such a scathing review. His business revenue increased.

Remember to properly identify the problem by embracing it and savoring it.

Amid all the dizzying changes and shifts that have been happening around us, also try to remember the notion of creative destruction. According to many sources, the term "creative destruction" was coined by Joseph Schumpeter, an Austrian economist, in the 1950s. Also known as "Schumpeter's Gale", according to Wikipedia, we are informed that the "gale of creative destruction" describes the "process of industrial mutation that continuously revolutionizes the economic structure from within, incessantly destroying the old one, incessantly creating a new one". As a theory of economic innovation and the business cycle, creative destruction occurs when a new innovation or technology essentially renders obsolete a previous technology, system or innovation. Innovation and creativity in the economy create something new, which displaces something outdated. There are countless examples, but one that many people can likely appreciate is found in the obsolescence of video rentals. An entire service sector, that featured networks of video rental stores, based on the technology of the video cassette and DVD, was "destroyed" as the innovation of digital streaming services became the norm. In this example, many people point to Netflix as the culprit responsible for closing their local video rental store; yet it was that very same Netflix that stated out as a company that rented out DVDs (on a mail-subscription basis).

So creative destruction, while bound to happen, really does open opportunities that did not previously exist. The key is being able to adjust, and to tailor your content and promotional efforts to those new opportunities. Self-reflection asks us to pause, step back and assess the "lay of the land"; to identify problems and embrace them. The goal of that practice is to confirm that we are moving in the right direction.

13

In any company, regardless of size or structure (including self-employed, charities and non-profits), it is difficult to identify a function more important and pervasive as marketing. As David Packard, co-founder of Hewlett-Packard, once said, "marketing is too important to be left to be marketing department."

Marketing is about the very culture of the organization, its identity. Especially in the burgeoning world of digital reach, everyone is their own, or their organization's, "cheerleader". A 2017 article in the *New York Times* described marketing as "the art of telling stories so enthralling that people lose track of their wallets."

Marketing is actually so many things. It is often a mix of advertising and promotion, sales, communications, public and media relations, social media, branding, organizational culture, and research. In fact, all these things that constitute marketing are, in fact, "content creation" and "promotion". When people talk about marketing, they often distance those functions from what they do; implying that marketing is something that only a small group of people or a department are engaged in. The fact is, everyone is involved in their company's content creation and promotion; they are, therefore, part of the marketing mix.

It is for this reason that budgets and efforts dedicated to marketing, or content creation and promotion, should not diminish during times of challenging cash flow. A knee-jerk reaction in moments of austerity points to the "marketing budget", believing that a reduction in efforts to tell your story and let people know you exist will somehow improve the bottom line. In fact, during those times when cash flow is weaker, it is often the case that more money and effort ought to be dedicated to content creation and promotion. At the very least, such moments should provide opportunity to determine if there are more effective methods to tell your story, to re-evaluate timing or distribution of effort.

You may be part of a political campaign. Perhaps you are a co-owner of an online or bricks-and-mortar retail store. You might work in the front office of a sports team. Perhaps you hold a managerial position in a church administration. You might work as a bank teller. In each of these examples, regardless of where your positon is located in the organization's hierarchy, you are part of content creation and promotion: every time you speak to other employees or members of the team; every time you attend a conference; every time you speak with or meet your customers, voters, members or subscribers. Content creation and promotion are what you do, and constitute the critical components of what builds and maintains corporate culture or organizational identity.

14

Personalize your Presence

Since the early days of marketing and communication, companies realized it was more effective to reach customers through a personal touch. Lovely women and cool guys sold cars. Animated characters sold hamburgers. Celebrities sold everything from beer to food products. And an English lizard is the most popular pitchman today for life insurance. Remember, personalize your presence.

It's not just an endorsement; it's about giving your message a face and personality. Maybe that personality is you - it doesn't always have to be third-party spokesperson. As was pointed out in earlier sections, there is a reason why real estate agents plaster their mug shots on their lawn signs and professional profile cards. This is true whether you're a corporate company, a not-for-profit association, a political party or even if you're promoting your own services as a self-employed person. Give it a personality.

Focus on a Main Message

Too many people make the mistake of wanting to tell too many stories in a short amount of time and space. Remember, if people take one thing away from seeing your post, your ad, your animated graphic, or even your website, what do you want them to remember? Because there is only one thing they will remember - and that is usually only after multiple attempts at telling your story. If you want your listeners, readers or viewers to do something, make sure that it's easy and takes practically no time at all. A radio ad asking listeners to remember a phone number, slogan, company name, hashtag and website is not only too much information for the listener; it requires someone to somehow transcribe all that information (if they can remember it) - not exactly easy for someone to do if that radio ad were listened to while driving a car.

Don't Over-complicate Things

If you can't encapsulate your idea into the space of a lapel button, it's too complicated. More importantly, if you can't crystalize your thoughts into three, four or five words, then you probably are still a little fuzzy about the idea yourself.

Use Every List of Contacts You've Got

Grow your presence first with your existing contacts and networks. Introduce things through email to everyone you know. And ask each of them to do something specific and simple, like sharing your original message with three of their contacts. It all starts somewhere. Like the insurance sales associate we discussed in an earlier section, that person needs to think of at least 100 names of people that he or she knows. Those names are the preliminary leads for outreach, potential sales or recruitment. They are also the names that probably already reside within the category of trust, that place where your voice already has a level of influence and authority. Word-of-mouth is as important today as it ever has been.

Understand Where Your Messaging Works - and Where it Doesn't

While you may start out by coordinating your messaging on multiple social media channels simultaneously, you'll likely to do better on some more than others. Maintain a constant monitor on metrics every time you communicate something. Just because one of your products or projects received good response through one platform doesn't mean that level of success will be matched in another. Learn how and where you're engaging peoples' interest, and build on that potential.

Your Medium Also Tells Your Story.

You probably wouldn't try to explain the details of a Powerpoint presentation over the radio or through a podcast; this type of story is better suited to a visual medium, like YouTube, for example. Similarly, using a book to teach a music student how to play a new piece is probably not as effective as using an app or website that combines the printed word with video and audio samples. Identifying the most suitable medium can augment your content by facilitating an enhanced potential for someone's retention of your message. You'll ultimately hit their senses of sight and sound at the same time. This is particularly important for messages, projects or services that are more complicated and might need that extra teaching tool. So your choice of medium not only facilitates your message, but becomes part of the message itself.

15

Harvard University scholar, Ronald Heifetz, has published and taught extensively on the principle of "exercising leadership", particularly the practice of "adaptive leadership". Within that body of work, Heifetz explores a key method of dealing with change, challenge and how to move forward, something he calls "getting on the balcony". In order to gain perspective in the midst of action, one ideally wants to develop the skill of getting off the "dance floor" and going to the "balcony". It's a mental activity of stepping back in the midst of action and asking ourselves, "what is really going on here?" As we look ahead, by stepping back and standing on the balcony, what emerges? What possible issues might we be confronting?

Amidst the rapid-fire changes going on around us today, as well as the yet-unidentified future economic and social disruptors, we can anticipate several issues gaining prominence as we look ahead. Standing from the "balcony", let's consider the following issues that could impact content creation and promotion, whether positively or negatively:

Privacy concerns are being addressed through legislative measures around the world. The European Union, Australia, the UK, much of South America, Canada, the United States, significant parts of Africa, the Asia-Pacific region, and Mexico have enacted, or are in the process of enacting, legislative measures dealing with data and privacy concerns. Such measures affect how a company collects and uses information, including cloud storage, search engines and promotional activity in the digital world.

Accessibility issues are gaining prominence globally. In this context, accessibility refers to how usable something is for anyone with mobility issues, anyone living with a disability, as well as seniors. The needs of a user who has weakened or zero eyesight will be quite different that the person with 20/20 vision. A user without use of his or her hands would undoubtedly find text-to-speech and other audible applications quite beneficial. Users or customers for whom accessibility is critical represent a significant percentage of the overall population. According to UN estimates, those with disabilities and seniors, namely those for whom accessibility is critical, constitute upwards of 22% globally (that's the number, roughly speaking, in most Western countries; some global-south and lower-income countries might be higher). Furthermore, medical advances and healthier lifestyles are contributing to longer lifespans. In other words, a condition or disease that would have once ended someone's life at a relatively young age can now live a much longer number of years. This, coupled with the aging trend of many societies, suggests that this is a demographic group that demands attention. Telling your story, and knowing how to promote your content, to this demographic group suggests some initial challenges, but significant opportunities as well.

Mobile dominance will continue. More and more people will eventuate to predominantly mobile usage. As we discussed in earlier sections, China is at this point already. Things will change rapidly. The switch in Western counties is advancing a rapid pace. If you're not optimized for mobile, this should be a primary focus.

The trend of corporate rebranding and the changing of monikers show no immediate signs of slowing. What some refer to as the "cancel culture", this momentum is a sort of digital shaming. And, make no mistake, it is very real. Easily mobilized, anything today can be a target for boycott, shaming or simply being canceled. Corporate and political leaders are especially sensitive to this activity. As we discussed earlier, there will emerge some opportunity associated with this trend, with some companies embarking on long-overdue re-brands.

Gaming today is more than online gambling and electronic games. The audience of e-sports and virtual competitive gaming is estimated at around 495 million people. This audience is expected to grow substantially. Platforms like Twitch have shown to be early leaders in the field. The world of gaming suggests impressive opportunity for anyone in the world of content creation and promotion.

Zero click-through results are becoming more common. These occur when a search engine company, let's say Google, provides results that are sufficiently adequate such that the user doesn't have to click through to another site. Zero click-through practices keep the user on the primary site where he or she conducted the search query, with a zero percentage of users clicking through to the websites returned in their results. Close to one-third of mobile users never click through on their search results. The implications for promotional effectiveness are considerable.

Internet networks always require more speed and greater reach around the world. These two insatiable requisites of digital access are currently being addressed through something broader than 5G: satellite internet service. Both Amazon and SpaceX are working to advance space-based internet networks, called Kuiper and Starlink respectively. The plans entail launching thousands of satellites into orbit. Both companies then plan to offer subscription-based internet access anywhere around the globe. As of February 2021, SpaceX boasted more than 10,000 users of its Beta service. Greater access, higher speeds, a truly global reach of users and customers - this is a trend worth watching.

Podcasts actually find their origin in the 1980s, although they didn't really experience any degree of popularity until 2004-2005. There seemed to be a healthy potential around that time, then their popularity tapered off. Until recent years, that is. Podcasts can now be live; they can offer audio-only or video-included content. There are dozens of companies that produce, distribute or catalog podcasts. Celebrities are increasingly turning to the podcast as a means of content creation, and influencers are readily found in any podcast listing. Podcast revenue is currently estimated at $1 billion annually - a figure that should pique the interest of anyone working in content creation and promotion.

Virtual events have become a norm. Today, any given conference or meeting of international attendees is easily held virtually. The cost effectiveness of virtual events, and a general acceptance of the effectiveness of such approaches, will continue to drive innovation in this area.

So, standing from the "balcony" does not help us predict the future or what the "hit song" will be; but it certainly allows us the opportunity to see just a little further down the road. The challenges and opportunities identified by looking ahead will define who is an innovator and who is a follower, who is a leader and who chooses to use last year's methods because they worked well at that time.

Everything around us is always in constant motion, so dedicate as much effort and as many resources to innovating your content and forms of promotion on a daily basis. The job of content creation and promotion is always a job in progress.

After these reflections on creating and promoting content, let's turn to one of the most explosive phenomena in promotion, user engagement and the power of influence – podcasting.

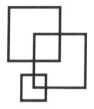

BOOK II

PODCASTING

Podcasting examines one of the most exciting explosions of technology and media, and how a podcast can become an essential component in the distribution of a message, the recruitment of members and volunteers, the organization and mobilization of a community, and how the podcast can advance causes and issues through the landscape of governance. *Content Creation and Promotion* is about the message, and *Podcasting* is about embracing technique.

PODCASTING

1

I t all started with a microphone? Actually, it all started with the Greeks (or so some say). The ancient Greeks were known for many contributions to western civilization. Among them were the use of public forums and amphitheatres for a variety of purposes, including speeches, debates, theatre, and oratory. But once a lot of people assemble into a single forum or amphitheatre, one quickly discovers the need to increase the volume of one's voice. They dealt with this issue in 5th century BC Greece by developing theatre masks with horn-shaped mouth openings that amplified the voice of the actor using the mask. It ended up looking like a customized megaphone. Essentially, it was a microphone.

Throughout history we have examples of how this communications technology developed, and the impacts it has made on our social interactions. In 1665, the English physicist, Robert Hooke, invented the "lovers' telephone", which was made of stretched wire with a cup attached at each end. Many kids called this a tin can telephone. In 1861, the German inventor, Johann Philipp Reis, developed a sound transmitter. That system was later refined by Alexander Graham Bell, which used a liquid transmitter whereby the diaphragm was attached to a conductive rod in an acid solution. All of these technologies transmitted the human voice from one place and in one form to another. The 1870s brought the invention of the carbon microphone, developed independently by David Edward Hughes and Thomas Edison. The carbon microphone is basically the early prototype of today's microphones. That prototype became the microphone used in a first-ever radio broadcast in 1910, one that featured a performance in the New York Metropolitan Opera House.

There have been massive advancements in the technology since then, especially with the advent of radio and television (both in production and in consumer engagement). Today, microphones are used wherever sound needs to be picked up and converted into an electrical format. Microphones are an essential part of any audio recording system. The microphone picks up the sound and converts it into electrical energy that can then be processed by electronic amplifiers and audio processing systems.

Radio

In 1886, the German physicist, Heinrich Hertz, identified a type of electromagnetic radiation that could carry information across space, from one place to another: radio waves. About a decade later, the first practical radio transmitters were developed by the Italian inventor, Guglielmo Marconi. A few short years later, radio began to be used commercially. As part of a test designed to determine how far radio waves could travel, Marconi in 1901 conducted his historic experiment that transmitted the first radio signal from southern England to the appropriately-named Signal Hill, located in St. John's, Newfoundland and Labrador.

The existence of microphones and radio transmission naturally opened the realm of broadcasting, which is essentially the transmission of audio information along the radio wave spectrum to radio receivers. It all sounds very complicated, but most homes in the commercial market eventually acquired a radio receiver, or more simply termed, a radio. Someone sitting in a studio in any given city or town could speak and deliver a message to an audience situated in their own homes (provided that home featured a radio receiver).

An interesting dimension about radio waves: while just about anyone with the appropriate equipment could start broadcasting to an audience of listeners, the waves themselves are shared by many users. Two or more radio transmitters in the same area attempting to transmit signals (let's say, a radio program) on the same frequency will end up interfering with each other. Radio interference resulted in poor reception (with a host of implications for any other signals transmitted over radio waves, including air traffic controls or emergency communications, for example). In stepped national governments to control, organize and coordinate the airwaves, as well as, in some instances, the content produced. We see these early attempts at regulation continuing in the form of the Federal Communications Commission (FCC) of the United States, the Canadian Radio-television and Telecommunications Commission (CRTC) in Canada, and the British Broadcasting Corporation (BBC) in the United Kingdom (fascinating fact: the BBC's original enabling license extended from the UK's General Post Office, which had original control of the airwaves because they had been interpreted under law as an extension of the Post Office's services).

Radio today has many frequencies, including AM (amplitude modulation) and its associated shortwave bands, FM (frequency modulation) which includes very high frequency (or VHF), as well as broadband, digital audio and satellite. Typically, someone, or some organization, wishing to send out programs, messages or other broadcasts would receive a license from a regulator to send their signal out on a specified location in a designated frequency.

Pirate Radio

Originally, as one can imagine, the field of radio prior to the entrance of governments and public policy was wide open to amateurs and hobbyists. In some jurisdictions, the amateurs were not banned, but given their own frequency spectrum. One should also be aware that naval communications once relied heavily on the use of radio waves (for communications and radar monitoring, for example), so any interference could have been catastrophic, especially during times of international conflict or war. Limiting the hobbyists to a dedicated spectrum was seen as a suitable measure to alleviating problems associated with interference. One might even say that, if not for the navies of the world, coordinated regulation, licensing and compliance measures of radio frequencies might today look very different. Naval necessities gave way to your favourite radio station? Yes, in a roundabout way.

The role of navies provides an appropriate segue to our next topic: pirates. Pirate radio surfaced as an issue when frequencies were hijacked, which was known as "wave piracy".

Another form of so-called piracy occurred when unlicensed broadcasters based their operations offshore and outside the jurisdiction of national governments, at times on an anchored vessel or marine platform. Free radio is another term that has been used interchangeably, particularly in the context of clandestine, unauthorized and unlicensed transmissions. So basically, if a broadcaster took the airwaves in an unauthorized way, or transmitted content that didn't follow a government's rules, they often fell within the category of pirate radio.

Technical requirements and equipment for establishing a pirate radio operation are not dissimilar to those of authorized and licensed broadcasters. Start-up and maintenance costs can be substantial.

Despite their differences, early radio and pirate radio both have some similarities to podcasts and podcasters.

Amateur or HAM Radio

Pirate radio is of the unlicensed and unauthorized kind; amateur or HAM radio is both licensed and authorized.

HAM radio is non-commercial, and is often used as a hobby or for personal training. The broadcasting activity of these radio amateurs is licensed, and limited to the use of small frequency bands. Globally, it is estimated that more than 2 million people are actively engaged in HAM radio operations, often associated through regionally-based clubs. HAM operators are required to comply with national and international codes and regulations.

The term, HAM, derives from the pejorative description given to those operators who, it was thought, lacked ability. However, the term has since evolved into one of a badge of honour by amateur operators, who have adopted the term as their very own moniker (which is an interesting example in branding).

While equipment and technical requirements can be modest, it is more common that the physical set-up of an amateur or HAM operator resembles that of a professional, commercial studio. A more-than-introductory degree of technical know-how is required, and costs for setting up a HAM radio operation, including annual licensing fees in some jurisdictions, can be prohibitive for many.

Despite the technical requirements and compliance measures, HAM radio enables that person with something to say, to be able to turn on the system, and start transmitting his or her message through the microphone. Certainly, some interesting similarities to podcasting.

Internet Radio

The medium has been referred to variously as net radio, online radio, streaming, and webcasting. Unlike other forms of radio, transmission via the internet does not require a broadcast license. While the content may be similar to broadcast radio or any of its variants, internet radio is actually not a broadcast. This medium is not wireless or reliant on radio waves; rather, it transmits from a computer and is typically available to any listener with internet or app access.

Nearly all traditional broadcast radio stations have a mirrored online presence. These entities are already licensed and regulated, and typically extend their compliance requirements to their online sites. While this allows any user anywhere to listen to the broadcast content of any given radio station, this is not, by definition, internet radio. Aside from the absence of licensing requirements, the regulation of internet radio rarely extends beyond customary website regulation (for example, privacy, copyright or accessibility). This is the key feature that frees content producers on internet radio to virtually do as they please: to create their own formats, playlists, points of discussion, whether profane or "safe-for-work". It's this quality and spirit of freedom that puts internet radio in a similar vein as pirate or HAM radio; it is also a quality that defines, and is echoed in, the world of podcasting.

Radio over the internet started in the early 1990s with the launch of "Internet Talk Radio" by Carl Malamud. In 1995 Scott Bourne created

NetRadio.com, the first internet-only radio network. In 1997, RealAudio entered the picture, and facilitated enhanced streaming accessibility as well as broadening the technology to deliver multiple formats. Keep in mind that this was developing during the early days of the dot.com boom. The user/listener experience was almost exclusive to the desktop or laptop computer, as the smartphone would not impact user and listener behaviour until well into the 2000s.

Although internet radio is not regulated in the same ways as traditional broadcast radio, some of the biggest challenges for these stations are royalty and webcaster fees.

In the early 2000s, internet talk radio was blossoming. It opened the opportunities for content producers to say what they wanted, however they wanted to say it. The need for technical knowledge was not as great as had been the case for other, previous forms or radio. However, the webcasting fees (that is, paying to have your program hosted on a server or streamed) were the challenging part. Additionally, as attractive as the internet is – particularly in its early commercial-use days – the challenge was identifying, locating and retaining a listener base.

The Feed: RSS Arrives

The issues of identifying, locating and retaining a listener base echo the challenges of content promotion: how does one minimize the chaos in the vastness of the digital universe, and make the content work?

RSS feeds were one of those answers in the realm of voice transmission. An RSS, or "really simple syndication", is a web feed that allows users to access updates to websites in a standardized, computer-readable format. The process of an RSS feed — the sharing or passing of content - is called web syndication. News aggregators have been common with RSS feeds for many years. A news aggregator automatically checks RSS feeds for new and updated content published online. The information is then passed from website to website or user. Today, any frequently updated information, such as blogs, news headlines and podcasts, typically use RSS feeds for distribution.

In 2000, the idea of attaching sound and video files to RSS feeds was being developed. In short order, audioblogging was born. More importantly, those same developers began toying with the idea of associating an RSS feed to an iPod feed, whic9h ultimately would move MP3 files to iTunes.

In 2003, a company called AudioFeast (later renamed PodBridge) had developed a method for providing episodic media, which enabled the user to download episodic audio content through desktop software and some portable devices. Around a year later, the first commercial podcast hosting service, Audioblog.com, was launched, and has since, in its later branding, hosted hundreds of thousands of podcasts.

The Technology of the Podcast Arrives

Around 2004, the word "podcast" had entered common usage among the development community. So much that by 2005 Apple added podcasting to its iTunes software and Music Store. That version of iTunes changed the landscape for podcasting. Provided a user had iTunes software on her or his computer, that user could subscribe to, download and organize podcasts. Apple software eliminated much of the need for users to employ a separate aggregator application. iTunes did it all. At the same time, Apple was also promoting the creation of podcasts using its own software applications, GarageBand and QuickTime. In fact, my first commercial podcasts were developed and produced using those very software applications at that time.

The term podcast had officially moved from the "techie" world to the commons. Podcast was named the word of the year in 2005 by the *New Oxford American Dictionary*, and it was added to annual editions henceforth starting in 2006. Even the President of the United States, then George W. Bush, became a *de facto* podcaster in 2005, as the White House website added an RSS feed to the President's weekly radio addresses.

Although the technology for podcasting production and distribution was never limited, Apple's active entry into the world of podcasting around the middle of 2005 represented a defining moment. First, the company offered users a way of "catching" podcasts. Second, they published their podcast directory. And third, they enabled the creation of podcast content by providing software that included tutorials on how to create and upload a podcast.

Of course, all this served to complement the landscape that featured Apple's 2001 introduction of something called an iPod, a portable digital audio player that sported a 5gb capacity (jaw-dropping at that time).

Yet the most compelling technology to change the landscape for podcasting has been the iPhone, Apple's smartphone first introduced in 2007. Smartphones had been under development since the 1990s, and the Blackberry, which preceded Apple's product, was globally popular for many years. However, the iPhone integrated everything in a way that contributed not just to the blossoming of e-commerce, but to today's reality of using a smartphone as anything but a telephone. Seamlessly accessing programs and episodes on a hand-held device, anywhere, at any time, has tapped into the ultimate authenticity of user experience.

The proliferation of smartphones has steered the explosion of app development and availability. Pre-installed podcast apps have played an enormous role in the continued growth of podcasting, beginning around 2014. Other dedicated, highly user-friendly podcast apps have appeared in app stores.

Yet it is the development and global popularity of streaming and associated streaming platforms that opened the door to a more fully integrated user experience for finding, listening to – and even creating – podcasts. Media and Communication professor, John L. Sullivan, describes the importance and significance of mobile technology: "Mobile consumption apps are critical to the infrastructure of podcasting because they provide a dual functionality as both tools of content discovery and consumption. Many of these apps are aligning themselves strategically and financially with discovery platforms to monetize their users' data…. Podcast mobile apps offer their own forms of interactivity, sociability, and content curation by highlighting within the app a unique constellation of content specifically designed for users." (John

L. Sullivan, "The Platforms of Podcasting: Past and Present." November 28, 2019)

Today, everyone has a podcast player in their pocket. More importantly, everyone has a microphone in their pocket. These technologies are ground-breaking.

Someone once said that humans love to listen to each other talk. If that's true, we can thank some of the technology developers from the past twenty years or so; or we can look back even further, and we thank the ancient Greeks for their know-how in helping amplify and transmit the human voice.

2

According to Podcast Insights, a research group, there were at least 850,000 active podcasts with more than 30 million episodes as of 2020. And, by using podcasting to broaden your content promotion, you want to bring that total to 850,001?

Before you rush out to purchase a podcast start-up kit (of which there are many available online), you'll want to consider several questions. The clarity of your answers will help determine what type of podcast is best for you.

Personal versus Professional

First, are you interested in speaking into a microphone, and sharing that content with the world, for personal or professional reasons?

Some people want to personally express themselves online, connect with like-minded people, and have fun. You might want to talk about your passions and hobbies, such as cooking and sharing recipes, or talking about small business issues in your local community. Others hope to develop new skills, such as learning audio editing software or public speaking. Some might even want to beef-up their CVs and online profiles.

In contrast, the professional podcast falls mainly into two categories: 1. creating a podcast on behalf of someone else or some organization;

and 2. associating the podcast with what you do professionally.

Some people excel at creating and packaging content for others; and, if you are one these people, this area of professional podcasts represents potential revenue generation (that is, monetization, which we will explore in more detail later).

The other type of professional podcast is the company podcast – the audio version of the corporate blog, so to speak. This can be internal or external. The corporate official could be speaking to employees and associates. The rise of remote work arrangements is perfectly suited for a professional internal podcast. Not only is the spoken word often more engaging, the internal podcast can help remote employees and associates feel connected and more aligned with their corporate leadership. The ease of production and distribution is also appealing for those people considering an internal professional podcast. The key to a successful podcast of this type is aligning the content and messaging with what employees find valuable. Regular podcasts of this type can also reduce the need and costs associated with periodic corporate training days, where vast bulks of information and content (quite often, too vast) are presented internally to employees and associates, say, at an annual staff conference. The internal podcast can replace part of that exercise, and often work far more effectively. The audience of the corporate podcast could also be external customers. This could be delivered from the office of the CEO, the elected official, or the business owner. The key here is creating something compelling to the extent that your listener wants to hear you again. In other words, that listener chooses to subscribe.

So, we have personal podcasts and professional (or work-related) podcasts. It's important to note at this point that both can be monetized. Advertising revenues from podcasts are expected to easily surpass $1 billion dollars (US dollars!) in 2021. We'll look at monetization and advertising revenue later. For now, it is useful to start considering whether your podcast will be mainly personal or mainly professional.

Another type of podcast that stands out from those discussed above is the celebrity show.

Celebrity status, whether global, national or local, is increasingly accompanied by attempts to extend "the life" of the persona (or monetize) through book publications, televised talk shows, and public speaking appearances. The podcast has also become a tool for extending celebrity (or monetizing). This type of podcast is part personal and part professional. Its defining feature is the existence of a brand that preceded the podcast. From famous movie actors, retired sports personalities, former radio DJs themselves, to individuals who for whatever reason enjoy a notable degree of fame and/or notoriety, the celebrity podcast works from an existing level of name and brand awareness among the public. And while this type of podcast tends to stand out among the other types, the celebrity podcast – and indeed, the celebrity himself – must be engaging to listeners to the extent that "return customers" are generated. (The term "celebrity" is not used in the more current, confining connotation of the word; instead, the use of the term "celebrity" here sources its etymology, specifically, of one who has a notable or public reputation, which could be a town mayor, a well-known local police officer, a real estate agent whose advertising adorns the park benches and local newspapers, or the owner of your neighbourhood diner or greasy spoon.

One final consideration on first principles: Is a podcast the most suitable medium for what you want to share online? As attractive as the prospects might be for someone imagining herself as a star behind the microphone, not to mention how fun it might be to make your home office look like a recording studio, there might be other mediums more suitable for you. Is your content primarily visual? Are you sharing a significant amount of information that requires the listener to make notes? While visual content can be attached to an audio podcast, that visual content might be better suited for a video presentation and to a visual medium (such as YouTube, TikTok or Daily Motion). Additionally, there are some podcast listeners who enjoy content away from their homes (in their cars, for example). If your target audience happens to be in that segment, then including information that requires manual transcription (such as, "get a pen and write down this address or phone number") isn't necessarily optimum for a podcast.

Know What You Want to Say and Why You Want to Say It

Upwards of 75% of podcast listeners report that they listen to podcasts to learn new things. The significant mass of users, then, see this medium as informative and educational more than they see it as entertaining. That said, the percentage of listeners who look for entertainment value in their choice of podcasts is also notable.

Are you diving in to entertain or to inform? Is the information in your episodes strictly your own opinion and slanted as a rant? Or do you intend to present a more balanced perspective that allows the listener to draw conclusions?

A good exercise that I have used with clients is to have them write out the trajectory of a potential episode, putting together a draft script, so to speak. After that, attempt to identify the topic of your next episode. Without scripting that second one out, are you at this point able to assign three to six words that describe your podcast? In other words, can you encapsulate the essence of what you want to say and why you want to say it into a pinback lapel button? If you can't, odds are that the focus is still somewhat hazy.

How Often Do You Want to Publish Episodes?

Like any content, a return visitor or customer expects to see and experience something fresh on a fairly regular basis. If there isn't any new content after, let's say two weeks, you've likely lost that person.

In a sense, this is also true for e-commerce websites as well as bricks-and-mortar retail locations. While a return customer does not want to be alienated by constant reorganization of products (that is, a degree of familiarity must be foundational), a return customer expects something fresh.

The average listener subscribes to approximately six shows, and listens to podcast content on average seven times per week. The average listener consumes about seven hours of listening time per week. Do you intend to be part of that listening pattern? If you do, your podcast station, or hosting website, will need new content on a regular basis. This is a commitment that podcasters need to make, otherwise they risk losing listeners and diminishing the base of potential engagement. We'll talk more about podcast content and publishing times and frequencies later in Book II.

What is Your Podcast Personality?

In other words, what is your brand? While this can evolve, and it doesn't always have to be firmly established at the beginning, adjusting your podcast's personality, or brand, is more difficult later in the process. At the very least, attempt to identify ideally who you are in the podcast listings and, more importantly, who you are in the listener's mind.

Are you an expert in some given field, be it a volunteer soccer coach or an experienced, loving mother and homeworker? Do you like to lecture, bitch and complain, or rant? Are you soft-spoken or rather loquacious? Are you at your best when engaged in conversation with others, or as a solo act?

One of the advantages of known personality and celebrity podcasts is that at least some key segment of the listening public knows who the person is (or, at least, who they think they know that person is), which transfers relatively easily into podcast branding.

Even without celebrity, though, everyone has something to say. Most podcast listeners want to learn and be informed. So, try and establish who you are, and what your podcast is, before you turn on the microphone.

Do You Have an Existing Infrastructure of Online and Traditional Properties?

It is important to take inventory in the early stages of development. In other words, are they any (and, if so, how many) websites or apps that are associated with you or your company? Do you distribute a personal or corporate newsletter? Do you have any existing promotion and advertising, be that in hard-copy flyers, direct mail, radio or television spots, window banners, billboards and the like?

Harness those properties to their fullest. While there are many excellent distribution platforms for your podcast, your existing infrastructure can serve as a "home market" foundation for your podcast. Wherever possible and appropriate, consider revising the messaging in each, and incorporating your podcast in some way. This infrastructure is the footprint of your brand; in part, it tells you how big your brand is.

Perhaps you have an online blog wherein you share recipes based on your love of Southern-style cooking. You now want to talk about your experiences in cooking, and perhaps include an interview with a guest. Wherever your blog is hosted it will have a basic feed that shares a notification of updates for subscribers. You might even have a separate email list, or a Messenger and Facebook roster of contacts. If you're really on the ball, so to speak, you would also regularly post photos of your culinary creations on either Instagram or Pinterest. This is your starting infrastructure. This infrastructure, and all the users it entails and engages, is what you need to build from; letting users know that you have a podcast, that you have something to say, and are now behind the live mic.

This existing infrastructure is also your basis for improved engagement, monetization and growth.

Do You Hope for Any Level of Active User Engagement?

One should hope so, given the tools and applications available to content creators in the 21st century. While there is a degree of user engagement through podcast and streaming platforms, the engagement often tends to occur in your base infrastructure. Promoting an upcoming episode through Twitter, Instagram or Reddit, for example, implicitly invites people to "like" or comment, to share or repost. Complementary user engagement in apps like those mentioned can help build your listener base by reinforcing a dedicated following of listeners or customers. If your podcast is monetized, active user engagement through your base infrastructure can also heighten the potential for revenue generation. At least half of podcast listeners state that they are somewhat more likely to consider buying a brand after hearing it advertised on one of their favourite podcasts.

Do You Have a Budget?

Planning and ultimately publishing your podcast require both financial resources and time. Both need to be budgeted. If your podcast is strictly personal and more of a hobby, a simple start-up kit of hard equipment typically does not exceed $100US, and in many instances can be substantially lower. The Do-it-Yourself (DIY) podcast for personal purposes has many free tools available. Creation tools and apps, publishing platforms, and distribution services can all be free-of-charge. Even the more sophisticated DIY audio engineering software (alternatively known as Digital Audio Workstations, or DAWs), such as Audacity, is open-sourced and can be obtained without any cost. Several basic websites and blogs at this level of podcasting can be free, and some are even customized with RSS feeds from your publishing platform, providing for automatic episode updates and transcription. One can even record, create, edit and publish a podcast today through the microphone in a smartphone.

More sophisticated podcasting can run much, much higher than the $100US cited above, sometimes entailing recurring production and editing fees, studio fees, hosting or distribution fees. Some former radio and studio staff have transitioned their services to podcasting. These can have a measurably higher level of sound quality, and certainly eliminate the time required in producing, editing and publishing.

The takeaway here focuses on determining how much time you want to, or can, dedicate to creating and maintaining your podcast; as well as paying a third party to putting it all together, or procuring the relatively simple equipment required, and operating from your home or your office.

As you move forward, remember that everything is about integration. All your existing efforts and commitments (for example, blogs, video content, newsletters, paid advertising) must work in harmony, not only with each other, but with your podcast. Too many companies still do not fully appreciate the importance of content and promotional harmony. Without a seamless integration of the properties in your foundation, you likely are forgoing significant opportunity of distribution, user engagement, and overall growth.

3

Putting any podcast together is not entirely dissimilar to putting together a radio or television production. The audience is always the first and ongoing focus. There must be a balance between entertainment and information, between levity and detail. There must be an idea, a topic, some complementary research and related content, often a written outline or script, an intro and perhaps a theme, an outro with perhaps another or similar theme, and, of course, the audio body composed of whatever it is the podcaster is saying.

Audio Body – Script it Out

Let's start with the audio body. Let's further consider that you, the reader, will be the podcaster – that person who will be speaking behind the live mic. For the purposes of this discussion, we'll also assume that you, the podcaster, have identified your focus, perhaps a name for the podcast, and what you will be presenting in your first couple of episodes.

Like so many other facets in life, preparedness can be critical to the success and effectiveness of our actions. Preparedness, or pre-production, in podcasting is no less important. While some podcasters seem as though they are free-wheeling without much of a focus, speaking to or with an audience nearly always requires preparation. For podcasting, that preparation, especially for the audio body of the episode, is an outline or a script.

Like a newspaper article, or an essay that you may have written in university, the body begins with an introduction, such as "In this episode we'll talk about" or "Welcome to Episode Number 1 of the ABC Podcast, where we'll explore issues related to…" Familiarize the listener with a short and concise topical overview. This is useful for new listeners as well as established subscribers, as the topical overview immediately confirms to the listener that the episode in question contains the content the listener expects to hear (this brief introduction can also be positioned in its own section, similar to a trailer or teaser, preceding the audio body or theme).

Some people script out their episodes verbatim, while others create an outline of main points. While there are advantages and drawbacks to each approach, it is essential to avoid sounding formulaic, mechanical or like someone who is reading. Find the approach that suits your preferences and style, but ensure that your delivery connects with the listener. While we'll talk more about style a little later, the importance of connecting with the listener recalls the discussion about knowing who you are in your podcast and what your online personality is.

Scripting is especially useful when guests or co-hosts participate, as well as for later transcription of the episode. Knowing who is speaking, and what each person is speaking about, is useful to outline ahead of time. Transcription of an episode is the written version of what was said. If those words aren't clearly thought out ahead of time, the written version will read in a rather awkward way. Why would any podcaster spend time on transcription? A written accompaniment can be performed automatically (with some manual proofing and editing required) in a number of programs. Audioburst is one example of such a program. So, there is no time involved in actually writing down the "proceedings". A written version is useful on a website, to appear as a blog, catering to a somewhat different audience (a reader as opposed to a listener). Podcasts about cooking, for example, can find added value in a printed transcription. Transcription also broadens the accessibility of the audio material to listeners with disabilities, again reaching and potentially connecting to a different audience. So, scripting achieves several objectives.

The audio body then ends with a closer. Much like closing words spoken by a broadcast reporter, the closer is a byline, of sorts. In a podcast, the closer is also a form of "station identification" and "channel access". For example, you might close out your episodes by saying, "Visit ABC Cooking.com for more episodes and information. This podcast is available on [identify your preferred streaming platform or primary platforms]. A special thanks to our guests, Mr. X and Mrs. S. I'm Mary Jane. Thanks for listening." This is a generic sample, of course, but can be adapted to just about any closer in any podcast.

Your episode now contains all the main content needed. That's the first step in pre-production. Print it out, if necessary. Read it a few times, then see if you're able to deliver the content without reading it.

Before we dive into a tutorial on recording and editing, there are a few other topics to consider.

Speaking Style

Not only does your speaking style help define who you are in the podcast (in other words, defining a part of your persona or brand), it is critical to connecting with listeners.

Most people are uncomfortable when listening to their own voices, especially in playback. This level of discomfort can diminish over time and with experience. The more comfortable you are with your content, the greater the authenticity and authority in your vocal delivery. The key is to avoid trying to sound like someone else. Use your own voice. Be yourself. Don't try to sound like an AM radio DJ or, for that matter, a 1950's broadcast reporter. Trends in styles have become less formal, notably friendlier and somewhat more intimate. The late actor, Lorne Greene, used to read the news on the Canadian Broadcasting Corporation nightly report in the 1950s. His delivery was consistent with the style of the time: forceful, louder, deeper and bold in tone, depth, timbre and delivery. His voice was so profound that he became known as the" Voice of Doom" (the moniker was also attributed to the seriousness or solemnness of the news stories, many of which focused on the Second World War). One hazards a guess that Lorne Greene's online (or on-air) delivery today might be substantively different.

Tempo

The optimal speaking rate, whether by a podcaster, Tuber, or radio host, is 150 to 160 words per minute. Some parts of the audio script will be better suited for a slightly faster tempo, while other parts can be coloured by a slower speaking rate, thus giving appropriate emphasis on words or sentences. Nervousness tends to increase one's speaking rate. It takes most people a bit time and practice to achieve a naturally slower and even speaking tempo. Try to avoid the "word race", the quick dash to condense as many words as possible into a given amount of time. Excessively higher speaking tempos can be uncomfortable for many listeners, and, at best, are probably left to the actors in the television show, *Gilmore Girls*.

Copyrights and Actionable Issues

Always aim to be original. If you reference other brands, use music or sounds that may be owned by someone else, do your homework and confirm their status, possibly even reaching out to the registered owner for permission. It is quite easy to download samples of well-known audio logos, themes or songs, and tempting for many to layer such content in the background of discussion. Understand that to do so can be legally actionable. Make it simple, and avail yourself of the free audio loops available, such as though DL Sounds or freemusicarchive.org. The BBC also offers a library of sound effects at https://sound-effects.bbcrewind.co.uk/. On a related note, exercise caution when speaking about people, products, companies or organizations, as one would in a public presentation or any other public discourse.

4

Where do we find some of the most active podcast listeners? According to a few studies in 2021, South Koreans, Spaniards and Swedes top the list, followed by Australian, American, Italian and Canadian respondents who state that they had listened to at least one podcast in the previous month.

Podcasts are growing in the number of programs available, in the number of listeners, and in the frequency of consumption. Today, podcast equals growth.

So how does a budding podcaster, with a brand new program and a handful of episode ideas, attract attention? How does one maintain that attention, retain listeners, convert listeners into subscribers, and build a potential foundation around the microphone? How does one promote this wonderful content bursting with potential?

A useful starting point, before we dive into a discussion of growth initiatives pertaining specifically to podcasts, is to address the concept of brand development and growth. The dimensions and techniques of brand development (which is really content creation and promotion) apply to nearly all online and digital activity.

It is highly likely that you, the reader, has a resume or CV, and that this "snapshot" of your life's work is probably extrapolated in some form on at least one social network (such as LinkedIn, Indeed, or Facebook). If you fall into this category, then you have already engaged in personal branding.

Put simply, personal branding is about promoting yourself in ways that establishes credibility and authority. The exercise helps position yourself as a leader or an expert in your field of endeavour, and it lets viewers of your profile get a glimpse of who you are and what you're all about. Hence the importance of concise, yet fulsome, bios leading-off your online resume, or those that are attached to a Google profile. It is this information you ideally want to appear in someone's search results about you.

Personal branding is not unlike branding a product, service or organization, in that the exercise is ongoing, requiring monitoring, nurturing, improvement, reinforcement, and, sometimes, repairing.

In a word, it's all about reputation.

So how does one go about defining and promoting a reputation? There are several steps in the process.

Knowing your competition (or, at least, those offering content in a similar genre) provides information about how others have defined their niche and expertise, reputation and brand.

What are the results when you search either for your name or the name of your podcast? Make sure that there are updated bios that reflect the reputation you aim to share with others.

Complementing your podcast with published articles (and don't overlook local community newspapers), contributions to expert panels, regular posts of written content on your website or blog, posts of related images, positive ratings from others, ratings you provide (for example, an online review for a book on podcasting), links to, and from, sites or podcasts that are within your realm of like-mindedness, or inclusion in Wikipedia (where appropriate and feasible).

Patience is a key factor in this process: content development, outreach and online results can take weeks, and sometimes months.

What if someone already has some level of "celebrity" or "notability", and the associations are negative? While some negative online content is difficult, and sometimes insurmountable, to remove, "push-downs" and "improvements" can be made, with results measurable within weeks. A "push-down" is a method of pushing negative content and search results lower, ideally with the aim of removing such content from the first page of results. An "improvement" is a method of improving online reviews and associated ratings. If, for example, a podcast has received multiple one-star reviews, there are methods to improve that rating to three or four stars. "Improvements" tend to take a little longer than "push-downs", often showing results in timeframes measured in months.

Finally, some people and organizations can avail themselves of the opportunities generated through Wikipedia. It should be stated with caution that, while Wikipedia is an excellent reference that helps promotional efforts, it is not – and should not – be considered as a promotional vehicle in and of itself. Wikipedia is an encyclopedia. So, any new Wikipedia page must have "notable" references, without which the page will be quickly removed. Notability on

Wikipedia refers to references that have their own Wikipedia pages, and not simply notations in other social media pages or personal websites, or public relations materials, such as media releases. Some of the above-mentioned examples, such as local community newspapers, can represent one source of notable references, especially if the published article in question is about the podcast or the podcaster. Rack up eight to ten of such notable references, and the podcaster just might be eligible to have his or her Wikipedia entry.

These are measures generally associated with any online branding and reputational campaign. Now let's consider several measures and techniques tailored for podcasters and their content.

Sharing and Measurement

A podcaster must continually share both the existence of the podcast as well as the individual episodes. The act of sharing is fundamental to the successful promotion of content. Measurement of activity and engagement, the metrics of the podcast, must be monitored on a regular basis. These two ongoing processes inform the podcaster about the effectiveness of publication cycles, distribution, content and engagement (to name a few). Ongoing sharing and measurement also reveal, for example, if the episodes are finding an audience with South Koreans or Canadians, or whether active user engagement is higher in Italy or in Australia.

Getting the Show Out There - Where Else to Publish

Anchor, owned by Spotify, is one of many highly user-friendly and free options to consider when starting. First, Anchor distributes to several podcast streaming services. Second, Anchor's reach also includes podcatchers and aggregators. In other words, some of the initial legwork in getting the podcast out there is taken care of by Anchor.

It is essential that a podcast be captured by catchers and aggregators. A podcatcher, or podcast client, is a computer program used to download various media, typically via an RSS feed. Podcatchers collate and catalog podcasts (aggregating them) to be collected as new episodes are released, rather than individually seeking out podcasts for consumption. When Apple added podcatching to its iTunes software in 2005, it became the *de facto* most popular client.

As a first step (and one that is handled at a basic level by Anchor) it's important to confirm that your podcast is captured. A few examples where it should appear include Overcast, Stitcher, Downcast, Podcast Addict, Pocket Cast and Castro.

As a podcaster, you can also reach out and contact companies directly, asking that they receive and list your program. The process is simple: usually an email will suffice, providing key contact information, RSS and website information, and basic details about the podcast. Although Anchor's distribution is decent, some platforms, like Apple, TuneIn, Amazon, require separate outreach by the podcaster.

Some of the common sources and streaming platforms for podcasts include: Apple Podcasts, Google Podcasts, Spotify, TuneIn, Amazon Music, Podchaser, PodBean, RadioPublic, Stitcher, Castbox, Overcast, Podcast Guru,

OwlTail, Blubrry, Listen Notes, Vurbl, Pocket Casts, and Himalaya.

Sharing and Monitoring

Use every list of contacts you've got. Never underestimate your existing contact list. As we considered in Section 11 of Book I, *Content Creation and Promotion*, that list is much bigger than most people assume.

Grow your presence first with your existing contacts and networks. Introduce things through email to everyone you know. And ask each of them to do something specific and simple, like sharing your original message with three of their contacts. It all starts somewhere. Like the insurance sales associate described above, that person needs to think of at least 100 names of people that he or she knows. Those names are the preliminary leads for outreach, listeners, subscribers and user engagement. They are also the names that probably already reside within your sphere of trust, that place where your voice already has a level of influence and authority. Despite the world becoming more digital by the day, word-of-mouth is as important today as it ever has been.

Get to know where you do well with your episodes - and where you don't.

While you may start out by coordinating your distribution and outreach on multiple social media channels simultaneously, you'll likely to do better on some more than others. Maintain a constant monitor on analytics every time you communicate something. Just because one of your episodes received good response through one platform doesn't mean that level of success will be matched in another. Learn how and where you're engaging people's interest, and build from that potential.

How and Why to Claim

What does it mean by "claiming" a podcast? At its basic level, it means that you manually find your podcast listed on a given platform, and register yourself to access metrics and analytics about downloads and streams of the episodes within that platform. Some of those details include critical information, such as knowing if a listener completed the episode or dropped off prior to completion; or how many episodes were accessed and the order in which a user chose to download or stream the episodes. Claiming a podcast can facilitate analytics that are more informative and instructive to the podcaster as he or she constantly monitors listener activity.

Launch with Inventory

In launching a podcast, it is best to have a minimum of three episodes complete and ready for immediate publication. Even an internal corporate podcast should imply a publication schedule by indicating topics for upcoming episodes. This demonstrates a track record with a selection of content, and depth and breadth of experience. An inventory also helps elevate a listener's interest.

Optimize Social Media. Get it Everywhere

Your new podcast is potentially one of the most exciting developments for you, whether the focus is personal or for business reasons. The podcast is also an opportunity to complement your existing promotional efforts (whatever products or services you might offer). However, not one person will know that it exists unless you constantly inform and remind as many people as possible.

You probably already had at least one active social media account (whether for personal or professional purposes) prior to embarking on podcasting. Your new podcast should be sufficient reason to broaden the social media reach, and fully engage all social media.

Announce the launch of the podcast itself. Announce each new episode. This activity must now be ongoing and routine for the podcaster.

Personal or corporate (or intranet) sites should reflect the availability of the podcast, ideally with an archive of previous episodes. Complementary blog sites, such as those now available in the Anchor-Wordpress arrangement, can serve as a dedicated access point. Let your contacts on Facebook and LinkedIn know about new content. Reddit, Instagram and Twitter also represent excellent options for outreach and promotion.

Discord servers are used by many podcasters to promote content. A discord is a VoIP (Voice over Internet Protocol), instant messaging and digital distribution platform designed for creating communities. Users communicate with voice calls, video calls, text messaging, media and files in private chats or as part of communities called "servers".

YouTube also represents a promising destination for some podcasts. Your complete audio file can be converted and uploaded to your YouTube channel. A simple way to do this is through Tunes to Tube (tunestotube.com), for example. The audio can be accompanied by still images or some basic moving images, even a stationary logo. Depending on the topic and content, a podcast channel on YouTube can attract considerably more listeners than dedicated podcast apps. YouTube is also in the processing of formalizing podcasts in its realm – evidence of the growth and influence of podcasting.

These are all free-of-charge options for helping to promote and to grow your podcast. Most of these options also offer paid promotional opportunities, each of which should be explored by the podcaster.

Consider a Launch Event.

Whether in-person or virtual, a launch event can represent that celebratory "champagne moment", much like a book launch, a film launch, or a product launch.

Some events help raise money to underwrite growth via paid promotional options. All such events represent the tried-and-true method of promotion: word-of-mouth. An event featuring 100 of your personal and corporate contacts can contribute measurably to the awareness of your podcast – provided there is a takeaway for those participating. People at such an event should be able to associate their favourite streaming platform or app as a listening option for your podcast. A hard-copy hand-out, say a bookmark or a fridge magnet, identifying how to access and listen to your podcast, not only has longevity, but is useful for the recipient. Another useful tip for participants at a launch event is to ask them to share your content more traditionally (by email, for example, with three key contacts), as well as via their preferred social media channels.

The key to a successful launch event is identifying what you want people to learn from your event, and what you want them to do after the event.

Use Your Podcast Intro as a Promotional Tool

Consider adding a short, snappy "primer", one that lets a first-time listener absorb the essence of your podcast (not just that specific episode) in ten seconds. The intro immediately educates the listener about the content of the podcast.

Leverage Your Guest's Audience

If your podcast features guest content, consider where and how that individual reaches and engages with people. A guest might mention the episode through her personal or corporate newsletter. A guest might also promote the episode through his social media, directing his audience to the podcast.

Offer to be a Guest on Another Podcast

Just as you might reach out to someone else to participate as a guest in your program, it can be equally useful to reach out to other podcasters and offer yourself as a guest. As a podcaster, you have a certain expertise or, at least, a well-developed basket of information and opinions on one or two topics. Keeping abreast of the content of like-minded podcasts helps a podcaster alleviate redundancy in content creation; knowing who is out there and what they're saying can also help you identify who might be interested in collaborating. Podcasters are usually on the lookout for good content, and reaching out in such a way often represents a welcome gesture.

Positive Reviews

Reviews are a guiding reality of today's digital and online world. The number and quality of reviews are critical to the success of an online product or service. This cumulative digital endorsement is just as important for podcasts. A high number of positive reviews, be they "likes", "up votes" or "stars", often helps usher a potential customer, or listener, closer to learning more about the content, product or service. Encouraging others to "like" a video, an app, or podcast, is now commonplace. Yet, the majority of users tend not to post a digital endorsement. So, some content creators use incentives to stimulate action. Provided the user genuinely likes the content, some content creators will dangle an incentive for the user to take action and post the endorsement, perhaps by offering a free product, reduced service fee, or some type of merchandise.

Connect with Other Content Creators, Podcasters and Influencers

Reach out to influencers or content creators to see if they will reference or mention your podcast. This method is typically used by creators and companies when launching or reinforcing a product or online content. The terms and conditions for each influencer and other content creators will vary, so a bit of outreach and legwork is required. That said, a reference or endorsement of your podcast by an influencer with tens of thousands upon thousands of followers might contribute to growing your podcast.

Growth of your podcast opens greater opportunity for monetization.

That said, there are some podcasters who do not desire growth. Some podcasters create and publish content for purely personal satisfaction or edification, even to learn new skills (not entirely dissimilar to HAM radio operators). Other podcasters, like a corporate CEO launching an internal podcast, are looking to identify ways to more effectively connect and engage with staff, as well as to augment or replace existing communication methods. Some podcasters simply want to reinforce the strength and connections of an existing community. Then there are those who don't care if anyone at all is listening to their content; podcasters who hold strong opinions about issues, and use the podcast as a soapbox or a rant. In fact, there have been instances when a podcaster's program has become so popular and successful, reaching ever-greater numbers of people than ever imagined, that the podcast shuts down.

Growing your podcast should not constitute a goal for its own sake. Identify if growth is appropriate for you, as a podcaster, and for the content you are presenting. Growth requires a monitoring of numbers and various analytics; but growth, if desired, should be identified at the outset as a primary measure of success, or whether there are other, more suitable measures of success for your podcast.

5

Spotify is more than just an app on your smartphone. Spotify Technology SA is sufficiently capitalized to have made history: signing a $100 million, three-year deal in 2020 with Joe Rogan (*The Joe Rogan Experience*) to exclusively host his podcast, making this the largest amount of money paid for distribution rights of any podcast.

Most podcasters don't fall into this category – yet. In fact, while revenue opportunities exist and are growing, there are not many podcasts that started out with the aim to make money. It is critical during the first stages of development to first build and grow an audience. Once the seed of that audience takes root, monetization becomes a very real option.

Today, it is common for podcasters to have sponsorships. This takes the form of the podcaster reading a short advertisement for a product or service. Some services, like Anchor, offer a fully integrated sponsorship model that allows the podcaster to record an ad, have that ad placed appropriately before, during or at the end of the podcast, and (for US podcasters) receive payment based on listening rates (or CPMs). Overall, ad revenue from podcasting grew more than 50% from 2017 to 2018. Those numbers have since increased exponentially.

Increasingly, these trends, coupled with the exponential increase in downloads, have caught the attention of the business world. The sheer (and growing) volume of podcasts, plus the fact that programs and episodes are tagged and categorized, complete with measurement tools and informative data, represents an attractive opportunity to reach defined user demographics.

The more the podcaster understands his or her audience, and how that audience accesses and interacts with the podcast, the greater the potential for monetization.

Analytics

Increasingly, podcast platforms offer a host of integrated tools, including analytics. These data are easily accessed via a company's smartphone app. Basic measurements include total number of listens and downloads (measured by day, week, or longer timeframes); total number of listens and downloads per episode; audience details, such country, region and city of origin; listening platforms used by the audience; age and gender breakdowns; and total number of subscribers (which is the more active and committed category of listeners). More sophisticated measures include details about referrers, clicks, search terms, drop-off points and rates, content that was skipped in an episode, tempo of play (normal, slowed and sped up), and levels of audience engagement measured by likes and comments.

With data like these a podcaster is given the opportunity to refine his or her content and promotional efforts – and earn a podcasting income. Businesses have the opportunity to finely-tune promotional and outreach efforts for their products or services to well-defined market segments in ways that few other mediums can provide.

Monetization

Podcast monetization is simply a buzzword that means making money from a podcast. There currently are two main ways to generate podcast revenue: 1. Direct monetization and 2. Indirect monetization.

Direct monetization refers to the generation of revenue from the podcast itself, whereas indirect monetization occurs when the podcast is used as a vehicle to sell other products or services.

Direct

There are several direct methods through which to make money from your podcast itself.

Donations are fairly common among creators across a broad spectrum of content. The content offered by creators includes video, audio or a similarly artistic form of content. The creator simply asks visitors, listeners or fans to consider making a small donation. The use of a PayPal button and accompanying account is one of the simplest ways to facilitate the donation. Perhaps surprising to some, this form of revenue generation shows some levels of success among content creators, including podcasters, especially if the potential donor finds value in the content and is confident that his or her donation will help produce more content.

Sponsorships, by far, represent the most common direct way of making money from a podcast. Some platforms will help coordinate sponsorships for the podcaster. All that is needed is an agreement with a sponsor. The sponsorship takes the form of a voiced narrative about the product or service, such as "this episode is brought to you by". These are short ads, usually not exceeding ten or fifteen seconds, and generate sponsorship dollars based on the frequency and total number of listens. Podcasters often charge different rates for ad placement (where it is heard in the episode) and ad frequency (the number of times the ad is played during the episode). Clearly, a substantial audience base is important to attract potential sponsors.

Paid Podcast Memberships can generate direct dollars. Much like a club or fee-based services, listeners or audience members are given the option to pay to receive more. The basic episode can represent the free-of-charge version, while more exclusive content or access requires payment. Many apps and online services operate on this model: employing a free version to help grow the base, and generating revenue through enhanced offerings (many anti-virus software programs, for example, operate on this principle). Many podcasters who employ this method of revenue generation use Patreon, which is a membership platform that provides business tools for content creators to run a subscription service. It helps creators and artists earn a monthly income by providing rewards or perks to their subscribers.

Custom content can also serve as an attractive vehicle to generate money. Ad-free podcasts, like any ad-free content in the digital world, can generate added revenue in a direct way. Some users don't mind the ads; while some actually enjoy them. In contrast, there is a paying public who prefer their content streamed without interruption or product pitches. This is a form of custom content. Another form of custom content that can directly monetize a podcast is found in audio material of a nature that is similar to the "extras" on a DVD or Blu-ray (for those who remember such "antiquated" technology). For example, let's say that your episode focuses on the release of a new music album, including reviews, song samples, discussion of the liner notes, etc. This is the free podcast content. If a listener is interested in that episode, then that same listener might be interested in something a little extra, perhaps an uncut recorded discussion with members of the band. This is custom content, and can contribute significantly to direct podcast monetization.

Indirect

Indirect monetization is used by many podcasters. Indirect ways of making money from your podcast include the following:

Selling products can offer an interesting form of indirect podcast revenue. Any merchandise associated with the podcaster is a potential product, including books, hats, t-shirts or bumper stickers. The podcast referenced at the beginning of this chapter, the *Joe Rogan Experience*, allows listeners to click into an online store. Of course, like many products available online, the user purchases each unit on-demand, so there is no unnecessary inventory on the podcaster's end.

Public speaking is a natural extension of the podcast, and some podcasters – especially those who fall in the "celebrity" category – have availed themselves of this indirect way of monetizing their content. As mentioned earlier, nearly every podcaster becomes a de facto expert in his or her topic. Sharing those experiences and that expertise in a larger, public forum - for a speaker's fee – can generate notable amounts of revenue.

Access to events (virtual or in-person) can be attractive for some podcast audiences. This form of indirect monetization occurs when a podcaster creates an event around the larger issues and topics of his or her podcast. The event can include special guests, keynote speakers, meet-and-greet opportunities, etc. Some podcasters have honed-in on such opportunity, hosting revenue-generating events (that also reinforce the promotional outreach of the podcast itself) on semi-annual and annual cycles.

Affiliate and partnership programs can be a simple way to indirectly generate modest income. The podcaster signs up with a given company. After a listener of the podcast uses the referring links, and subscribes to the affiliate, the podcaster receives a payment. The podcaster is the referrer, and facilitates new subscribers or sales for the affiliate. For example, Audible.com pays $15 for each new trial membership generated by the referring podcaster. Audible asks that the podcaster promotes a 30-day free trial of Audible; with a custom link provided by the podcaster. Through that link, the listener then arrives at the Audible landing page. Listeners get access to a free audiobook, and the podcaster generates payment for each trial membership secured by Audible. According to *Podcast Magazine* (February 2020), 18% of podcasters generate income through promoting products as an affiliate.

Generating revenue, or monetizing your podcast to become a revenue stream, is something that many podcasters are doing quite successfully. The note of caution is this: like any other exercise in developing a revenue model, the podcaster's efforts to monetize his or her content requires a business plan or operating and growth plan. It is essential to identify expenses, a potential audience, and plan for audience growth, the timing of implementing the monetization model, the revenue expected, and the sources of that revenue. While not endorsing any particular company, a podcaster interested in monetizing podcast content might consider working with an ad network, such as Rockable.co or True Native Media. RedCircle, a company that bills itself as a one-stop shop, also offers features that help monetize your content. Generally, companies like these help match podcasters with businesses interested in advertising. They also help create advertising campaigns, something a typical podcaster might not hold a lot of expertise in, and structure pricing models around CPMs (cost per 1,000 listeners) that can be quite attractive.

6

While there are many ways to apply a revenue model in order to monetize your podcast, there are some podcasters (both personal and organization-based) who are not creating and sharing content to make money. Some are out there simply to have fun or learn new skills, and have little regard for the composition and quantity of listeners. There are many others who publish podcasts on behalf of non-profit or charitable organizations, educational institutions, community clubs and associations, church and religious organizations, civic organizations and political parties/candidates. These podcasters often monitor the analytics of their episodes and listener base as much as those who do so for potential monetization; but those who fall in the not-for-profit realm are usually deeply concerned about building subscribers, recruiting listeners and growing a loyal audience for the broader purposes of outreach and recruitment. One of my earlier podcast projects in 2006, produced for a Canadian national non-profit, focused on the daily challenges, stories and joys of young man living with Cerebral Palsy, who required the use of a motorized wheelchair for mobility. The podcast was created to advocate, raise awareness and engage grassroots support for social issues.

Share your Organization's Stories

Storytelling is central to the world of non-profits, not-for-profits and charities. The story about the cause, the need, or the recipient of the organization's work consumes the lion's share of traditional communication and outreach by such organizations. Think of any given audio or visual commercial. The story, the narrative, focuses on the poverty in a remote village, for example, or the saga around stray dogs and cats. The story is the hook that captures attention, secures appeal and opens opportunity for donations.

Podcasts, at their core, are stories; and podcasters are storytellers. The podcast is ideally suited for the world that seeks to build memberships, recruit volunteers and supporters, reinforce a solid and loyal following, engage interested parties, and secure donations.

A podcast for a local community service club would naturally focus on storytelling, at least in several of the program's episodes. The stories convey to listeners how the service club engages with and impacts the community. The creative applications are virtually endless. Episodes can include participation by representatives of local businesses who work with and help support the club – which could be converted into a model of sponsorship. Content could also include interviews with community members who describe in their own words how the club's work helps improve the well-being of the community. Guests (such as those who are near-and-dear to the club's work) can convey the passion that is so effective for podcast outreach.

For the world of charities and non-profits, use a podcast to share your organization's stories, creating additional opportunities for sponsorship, fundraising and volunteer recruitment.

Elevate your Organization's Profile as a Go-To Source of Expertise

While branding and the development of organizational persona are critical to differentiate one organization from another, it is equally important to guard against approaches that are too narrow in scope and application. For example, an organization that seeks to raise funds for research in a given area of cancer could enhance their organizational profile from strictly "cancer" to broader community betterment and well-being. Presumably, such an organization would have a significant repository of information and stories by and about patients, families, survivors and social networks. In addition, such an organization would have a unique wealth of expertise on the implications of job and career prospects, poverty, clean-air initiatives, or recreation funding by a local government, to name a few areas. The podcast is that valuable tool in commenting on such areas, broadening the profile and importance of the organization, and potentially enhancing the organization's status to a Go-To source of expertise. Suddenly, that organization, which was focused solely on raising funds for cancer research, is now a source of expert opinion for the media, government committees and town-halls, on a much broader range of related issues.

So, use a podcast to comment on a host of issues that are indirectly related to your organization's work, and broaden your organizational expertise.

Content can be Re-purposed

As many non-profit representatives can attest, the time, effort and money expended on outreach sometimes fall flat. Perhaps donations at a special event did not meet expectations. Perhaps an event beyond one's control (a pandemic, for example), has impacted how the public prioritizes donations, volunteer time, and notions of "need". Yet, the excellent work that went into developing the content for that special event, or for the public service announcements that had to be pulled due to an unforeseen pandemic, can still be used.

Repackage the content into a podcast episode or two. In turn, content from the episode, including listener feedback, can be re-purposed for use in other online properties, such as a traditional blog. In other words, the podcast creates the opportunity for integrated re-purposing of content.

View the podcast as a source of information, as well as content that can feed directly into your organization's existing inventory of promotional and outreach tools, and vice versa.

Generate Volunteers Using the Passion of Existing Volunteers

Whether the organization is a political campaign or a church group that coordinates community events or food drives, volunteers are needed, and sometimes numbering in the hundreds.

A podcast can help attract and recruit volunteers - that essential, make-or-break source of human passion and labour. Episodes can be hosted by volunteers. Remember, a volunteer can be anyone: a student, a retired homemaker, a university professor, a local bank manager, or a local actor. Alternatively, episodes can feature or highlight the experiences and stories of one or two volunteers in every episode.

So, use your podcast as a recruitment and retention vehicle.

Engage Your Spokesperson

It is not uncommon for some non-profit organizations, especially of the charitable nature, to have a public spokesperson or campaign chair. Such individuals either have standing in the local community, or enjoy some degree of celebrity beyond the community. Some of these individuals send mass emails to potential donors, volunteers or voters; some appear in special public service announcements.

Seek to organize episodes that focus on the spokesperson or campaign chair, featuring a discussion of why that individual is so committed to your cause.

Published, distributed and integrated effectively, coordinating the organization's existing inventory of promotional and outreach tools, and that episode can have far wider potential than the organization's key base of support. Wherever the spokesperson has an audience or at least some currency, your podcast now has expanded reach.

Use your podcast to harness the reach and impact of a spokesperson, honorary or campaign chair.

7

Even if your podcast is a purely personal endeavour, with little or no regard to audience outreach, listenership or feedback, you can still benefit from user engagement by receiving suggestions for improvement. Listeners can help refine content, production techniques and the overall listening experience. User engagement can be an effective approach to enhancing the quality of your podcast and your personal podcasting skills.

In contrast, if you want your podcast to grow, regardless of whether your content is published for personal or professional reasons, then user engagement is critical to your success.

So, what is user engagement in podcasting? At its core, user engagement is the process and activity of communication between the content creator (the podcaster) and the recipient (in this case, the listener). User engagement can have the effect of narrowing the gap in the relationship between the content creator and the listener, building a more intimate and interactive audience experience.

An intimate and interactive audience experience can be important for several reasons: trustworthiness of the message (which is key for product or service promotion); likelihood of message propagation (when a listener shares the podcast); likelihood of listeners feeling part of a community (which is ideal for brand association); conversion of listeners to subscribers (which positions that audience as a market segment); and conversion of listeners to supporters/buyers (whether online or in a physical location).

The tips here are really quite simple.

Comments

When you publish, make sure that your content allows comments. More importantly, respond to those comments, sometimes as simply by indicating a "like" or "thumb's up". By doing so, you let that user know that you value the input, and that you consider that person's voice as an important contribution to the content. Ignoring listener comments suggests that only the podcaster's comments are legitimate, and this can create an unnecessarily arrogant ambiance in the podcast.

Dedicated Forums of Discussion

The podcaster can also create discussion groups as an extension of the podcast. Forums through Reddit, Discord, Clubhouse (to a degree) and Twitter (increasingly) are three examples of useful places to start. This form of user engagement is more time-consuming, as it can require the presence of a moderator. That said, for those podcasters who have the time, discussion forums are wonderful sources of ideas, as well as a well for listeners to feel part of something connected to, but exclusive from, your podcast.

Don't Just Monitor or Lurk

Visiting and watching the activity in any given social network, or on any given social media, represents a half-step. Go further: participate in such networks. The podcaster's participation in social media can generate listener affinity. It can also help reinforce the sense of audience community when a listener sees posts and commentary in his or her favourite social media.

The Listener's Voice Can Matter, Too

This is something that Anchor (for one) has leveraged. By allowing users to leave a voicemail through the podcast (specifically, wherever the podcast finds its home), the podcaster has a highly engaged type of listener, someone who is active and passionate enough to make a call and leave a message. That listener is a source of further recruitment, someone who can be "deputized", to engage in outreach and promotion (or social network moderating, as mentioned above). By leaving a message, that listener is also providing a possible source of content ideas for future episodes. That voicemail can also serve as excerpted content in a blog, or copied directly as an audio file into an episode that features the listener's quote. Treating listeners respectfully, by letting them know that their voices matter as well, is not only a good practice in user engagement; it is empowering for the listener.

The Effectiveness of Email

Research from Salesforce shows that users (or consumers) prefer to receive promo content through their email to a far greater degree than through any other form of communication.

Email is an effective way to encourage listeners to engage: to post reviews and offer feedback; to provide ideas for future episodes; and to ask questions that could be addressed in an upcoming episode.

Similar to the importance of one person listening to another via podcast, email is a direct form of communication that can enable or empower the recipient. It can also last longer than a text message. User engagement through email should never be overlooked or considered "old school".

Benefits of User Engagement Unique to Podcasts

Podcasts really do have special qualities. Like radio, listeners tune in because they enjoy listening to another person talking about something. Unlike radio, the podcast feels more intimate. Statistically, most listeners enjoy podcasts while listening alone rather than in a group setting. The more a listener becomes familiar with the podcaster (the voice, the nuances in pronunciation, tastes and preferences), the more likely that listener is to return and subscribe. Engagement helps reveal what information in a podcast is useful or interesting for the listener. And the more interesting and useful the podcast is, the more likely that listener (and potentially others that he or she informs) will rely on that podcast for those sources of opinion, information or entertainment.

Having a loyal following is something businesses consider attractive. That following is a definable market segment able to be captured within a given digital space. Ad placement and monetization represent one example, albeit a powerful one, of such benefits of user engagement.

Regardless of the aim of the podcast, engaging with the audience produces some of the key benefits associated with strategies for growth, promotion, monetization, improved content, or more effective production techniques. User engagement for a podcast can occur within the immediate sphere of the podcast (within an episode). Listeners can also be engaged with the podcaster in the indirect realm (social media, email, discussion forums). Podcasts are content. As with any content, user engagement (or listener/audience engagement) can help define both the success of that content, as well as the form that any future or ongoing promotional efforts might take.

9

Some podcasters prefer the self-produced approach, while others enjoy only recording the audio and leaving everything else to a service provider. Then there are those who want to have a podcast, but don't want to have to worry about anything except speaking into a microphone in a professional studio. There is no "right" approach, or "wrong" approach, for that matter. Whichever approach you take, keep it real and maintain the authenticity.

Certainly, one of the benefits of self-produced podcasts is a minimal flow of cash from your budget. The biggest benefit is the authenticity a self-produced approach can yield. Podcasts are among the most intimate of mediums, so any hint of inauthenticity can be very off-putting to the listener.

Professional production does not suggest an inauthentic outcome. However, such an approach can inadvertently distance the voice from the listener through excessive layers of "slickness". At this point, the podcast is no longer intimate. It's much like a small business procuring an award-winning cinematographer to produce a short promotional video for rotational view on Facebook: users can be – and have been – put off by the slickness and accompanying inauthenticity of the message. The company being promoted is a small business; and the "overproduction" and "slickness" results in a mismatch between product and message.

A note of caution: Some ventures into podcasting may suggest a dedicated function within your company. Some considerations include the possibility of at least one dedicated individual (internal or external) who (a) coordinates/creates content, (b) serves as a liaison with the podcasting service provider, (c) analyzes and interprets the listener analytics, and (d) moderates user engagement. The benefits generated through a podcast are significant and growing; and, depending on the approach taken to creating and sustaining that podcast, the budget can also be significant.

Whether you opt for a DIY or contract-out approach, identify what outcomes and deliverables you expect from the podcast, the podcaster and from the platform. Finally, conduct some comparison shopping to discover other podcast service providers, their features and their prices.

10

Some analysts caution that, without attracting and retaining newer generations of listeners, radio could eventually pass away, along with the existing generations of listeners themselves. A recent study from New York University highlights the pitfalls associated with this shift. Traditional radio has not engaged with Generation Z — people born after 1995. The authors of the study warn that radio will continue to decline in relevance unless substantial changes are made.

Radio remains popular for many people, and it is a powerful source of reference for others; but young people don't listen to the radio. So, a generation-based shift has occurred, one that was ushered in via the convergence of technologies. According to a 2016 Music Business Association study, young millennials only spend twelve percent of their listening time on radios; whereas on-demand streaming accounts for more than half of this generation's daily listening. Furthermore, young people aren't discovering new music or programs on radio anywhere near the extent to which they turn to sites like YouTube.

The habit of tuning into a terrestrial radio station while driving is also a target of change (perhaps decline). Newer cars increasingly are integrated for digital streaming, providing the listener even more opportunity to consume his or her favourite podcast content.

The increasing popularity and integration of digital assistants and smart speakers also contribute to the increasing popularity of podcasts. The Infinite Dial, a company that tracks device ownership, confirms that much of the upward trend in podcasting is at the expense of traditional radio. Their studies also show that radio ownership is dropping: since 2018, smart speaker ownership has risen 50% while radio ownership has dropped slightly.

11

On a stage or behind a microphone, the human voice reaches new levels of impact, and sometimes more meaningful depths.

The podcast is among the more recent additions to our communications inventory of how to use and share the human voice.

Unlike so many other forums in which the human voice is used to communicate, listeners of podcasts tend to consume audio content in a more intimate way. Most listeners report using headphones or earbuds when listening to podcasts. This can be a very intimate and immersive way to convey a message or deliver a narrative to a listener. The listener becomes one of the most captive at that moment. Here is a forum with one or a few voices speaking to one person at a time.

Beyond the advantages associated with digital freedom, the intimate, immersive and captive nature of the audience is an attractive feature of podcasts that many radio professionals would like to own. Couple this communicative power with the fact that podcasts, by their nature, are niche and reach an audience already accustomed to consuming content in niche ways. The content and the storytelling are all about the human voice. But there is a quality about the listening audience, the user at the centre of the experience, which still seems to defy definition for many.

In other words, perhaps we are learning that audio storytelling and communication – through podcasting - is more than about the human voice; it is also (and perhaps to a degree greater than we have yet understood) about the human ears.

It is the definable, more intimate and immersive user experience that makes podcasts attractive to a listener. Furthermore, the technology works around the user needs (the listening choices and methods) of the listener. In fact, the audience in podcasting is often conceptually viewed from the perspective of one person at a time. Radio, by its very nature, is more general. Radio tends not to conceptualize around a user or a listener, but rather for an audience. It casts in a "broad" way.

A final bit of advice. As you commence or reflect on your podcasting journey, step back on a somewhat regular basis, and ask if your audio content is doing what you want it to do. Routine self-reflection can only refine and improve the project. So always ask two questions, every now and then: Is your podcast achieving your goals? How do you know? Finally, save your episodes somewhere, and in a format and place external to your website or your podcasting host.

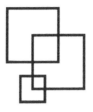

BOOK III

ADVOCACY

Advocacy, an Amazon Bestseller in early 2022, is also about amplifying a message for an social or political purpose, and of getting that message out there to its intended audiences. The use of audio outreach, particularly podcasting, can help maximize the effectiveness of any advocacy campaign. As a form of content creation and promotion, *Advocacy* continues the dialogue by focusing on the application.

ADVOCACY

1

S ocial advocacy, brand advocacy and political advocacy are three of the most commonly-used narratives in making change. Within those categories, and complementing each, are several other specific areas of advocacy: legal, bureaucratic, issue, budget, ideological, for example. Lobbying is a specific form of advocacy that is now legally defined in many jurisdictions internationally, a process that involves and focuses on holders of public office. Further distinctions and forms of advocacy are nuanced by whether the work is performed in-house as a function of a corporate or non-profit organization, and as an extension of the organization's mandate; contracted externally to the corporate or non-profit organization, but also directly linked to the mandate of the organization; or performed individually with no legal or technical association with any organization.

Key to any type or form of advocacy is the need to "navigate the circuitry". The effectiveness of advocacy, regardless of its type, form or purpose, is inextricably linked to one's capacity to navigate the system in question, as well as the players in and around that system.

Advocacy is not new. Advocacy in varying forms is as old as the concept and practice of persuasion.

Another feature of advocacy is the "transition effect" - when advocacy efforts have transitioned into institutions. Attempts to change outlook, policies, laws and administration were at the origin of many of today's institutions. *The Economist*, for example, was founded in 1843, not so much as a weekly news and opinion periodical, but as a mechanism to campaign for the repeal of Britain's protectionist Corn Laws (which, incidentally, was achieved three years later). The nucleus of American independence is found in a mass reaction to tax laws imposed on the American colonies by decision makers in Britain. It was only after unsuccessful attempts to persuade legislators in Britain to reconsider their landscape of governance did a more radical alternative emerge.

Advocacy also manifests within policy. For example, international trade policy is routinely used as an advocacy tool to advance human rights. Trade deals increasingly include labour-related provisions, child labour, forced labour and employment discrimination. Trade embargos, a tool of trade policy, have been used to address larger, more systemic social issues, as was the case with apartheid in South Africa.

Book III, *Advocacy*, will first flush out what advocacy is and how it is defined in varying, and sometimes confusing, ways. It will identify and explain sources of confusion around advocacy, specifically by discussing legal advocacy and lobbying. The discussion includes an outline of the importance and significance of advocacy, today and historically; practical matters, methods and techniques; the use of measures and metrics of performance; and use, advantages and disadvantages of working together, uniting in a common cause and joining forces; and some future trends, such as online and digital innovations, as well as the evolving connection between communications and policy.

First, a brief note on the use of terminology. Lobbying is legally defined, and a professional who engages in the practice of lobbying is usually required to register and report to the government (or governments) in a particular jurisdiction. Government relations specialists and activists who both engage in direct advocacy with public office holders may not necessarily be subject to the same levels of scrutiny and compliance; although they could be, depending on if their practices happened to have surpassed a legislatively-defined threshold (for example, number of hours dedicated to direct meetings with public office holders, or solicited versus unsolicited interaction with government officials). General public perception of lobbying would confirm that a professional working for a pharmaceutical firm, whose job is to influence or alter public policy, would likely be described and registered as a lobbyist; whereas that same professional whose work focuses on representing the interests of a charitable organization would likely be thought of as a government relations specialist, an activist or an advocacy professional. Somewhere between the two scenarios is the bank CEO who makes a phone call, if only once, to a finance minister to comment on budgetary measures, fiscal or monetary policy; yet this individual's job does not focus primarily on engagement with public office holders, and the conversation is intended to provide quick, direct advice from a sectoral technical perspective – yet that CEO would not likely be required to register as a lobbyist, since the phone call was a one-off incident. In each scenario the stakes could be just as high, and each organization has a legitimate role to play in informing public policy decision makers.

Government definitions offer some clarity in helping differentiate what constitutes an advocacy professional, an activist, a government relations specialist and a lobbyist. But the fact is that, regardless of title, they are all *influencers*.

2

Lady Godiva (yes, after whom the namesake of Godiva chocolates is inspired) was more than a woman of beauty, aristocracy, wealth and power. She was an individual (perhaps one of history's more famous of such) who took up the task of speaking for those without a voice. She recognized that something needed to be changed, an issue needed to be addressed, and she took up the cause. The stories only date back to the thirteenth century (when, in fact, she lived during the eleventh century), but describe Lady Godiva as having agreed to trade her clothing for lower taxes. In sympathy for the townsfolk, who were burdened by her husband's "oppressive taxes", she rode, naked, on a horse through the streets of Coventry as part of a "campaign" to convince her husband, the Earl of Mercia, to lower the taxes. Despite disagreement among historians regarding the authenticity of the story, the legacy today finds life in books, film, confectionary, statues and paintings – and in historical comparisons of advocacy.

The issue of taxation has long been central to advocacy. This is not surprising given that taxes often represent a tangible expression of the notions of fairness and equity in public policy and public spending. Interestingly, on a thematic scale, we probably find more threads linked to notions of fairness and equity when considering advocacy efforts. The core of the matter, though, is the changing of rules, regulations, processes or laws.

Why is Advocacy Needed?

We have electoral cycles which serve to confirm the personnel of many public offices. Why do we require anything more than selecting representatives or deputies during the official electoral cycles (municipal, provincial or state, or national)?

Lady Godiva's time typically was not characterized by electoral cycles or participatory democracy. Everything from monarchs and nobility to self-appointed rulers, dictators and despots, made decisions with little, if any, citizen input. If not for the occasional benevolence of the ruler, making a change to any given course of action (or proposing a new one) would have required at least one individual who had the ruler's "ear" (as was the case with Lady Godiva). Rulers generally did not seek input or opinion on the effectiveness and efficacy of their decisions.

Today, input and opinion are considered critical to the effectiveness and efficacy of most public policy measures. In the first (and obvious) instance, the next electoral cycle would displace a host of public office holders should the public deem their decisions and performance unsuitable or unsatisfactory. In the second instance, input and opinion provide technical expertise, and facilitate feedback on the potential impact of proposed measures.

Citizen input and opinion is one of the major reasons why governments receive (and sometimes solicit) representatives from the public to "speak up" and participate. Governments and legislatures often invite groups "in", usually as part of process of public consultation, to make deputations or to provide testimony at committee hearings, to promote a message or cause, and provide input and opinion. So, governments need a certain amount of advocacy from the public to create more informed and sustainable programs, services, laws, amendments, and the like.

Then there are those groups who want to make an impact independent of electoral cycles or public consultations. Often (but not always) falling into the category of lobbying, this type of advocacy finds life through an individual who knows how to navigate the system, knows how to reach the key individuals in the multiple mazes of government, knows whom to speak with, and how to get their ideas heard. This sort of advocacy sort can entail just about any type of issue or policy field, from procurement or pharmaceutical regulation to seniors' benefits and airline safety measures; and, as this is usually a paid form of advocacy, only those issues sufficiently financed will typically find sustained life.

Advocacy within Government

When we speak of advocacy efforts or campaigns, the focus on any exercise is typically a government entity of some sort, be it a department, ministry, board, agency or commission. This is not surprising, since it is government (at least in most societies today) that imposes and collects taxes, creates laws, public rules, orders, regulations and systems of governance.

Sometimes the advocacy lead originates inside governmental systems. This is usually a small office of government employees whose job it is to ensure that a certain bundle of issues is not neglected or negatively impacted by general government decisions and activity. Internal government advocates serve to amplify and apply a "lens test" to government activity. Applying a "lens" typically means looking at the spectrum of government programs, services, policies and procedures, and determining how positively or negatively all of this government activity impacts a certain group in society. Internal government advocates have been designated for seniors, race relations, indigenous issues, women's issues, children, and disabilities, to name a few.

Advocacy: Introduce. Change. Oppose. Eliminate.

The purpose and goal of advocacy, more often than not, is to introduce something new, to alter something that already exists, to oppose a proposed or existing idea or structure, or to outright eliminate something.

The "something" in reference could be many things, although encouraging an increase or decrease in spending on a particular measure is frequently the norm. In addition to promoting a change in the amount of money being spent on a particular policy area, there are many other focal points of advocacy: introducing climate measures, such as emission reduction targets; introducing the creation of a new national holiday; adjusting/altering immigration numbers; removing/eliminating certain behaviours or substances from a criminal code; adjusting/changing a speed limit for driving on certain roads or highways; or opposing a proposal to reform the electoral system.

Advocacy Surrounds Us

Some define advocacy as an activity by an individual or group that aims to influence decisions within political, economic, and social institutions. This definition is quite broad. Is a sit-in an example of advocacy? Is a protest an example of advocacy? Is a strike an example of advocacy? How about an election campaign? How about a child attempting to obtain an increase in his or her weekly allowance, especially when a parent is suggesting to the child to "speak to your mother" or "speak to your father"?

To the extent that a significant component of advocacy entails promotion, persuasion and encouragement, all of the above certainly could be termed advocacy.

But Not All Forms of Persuasion or Promotion Constitute Advocacy

There first must be an identified goal. Advocacy is less clear-cut when there is no goal; or when there are multiple participants in the advocacy process, but there is no common understanding of purpose or aim. Some so-called advocacy efforts are little more than attention-getters or public stunts.

Clarifying Definitions: How to Identify Advocacy

Advocacy is an activity by an individual or group that aims to influence decisions within political, economic, and social institutions, most typically those institutions of government. The activities of advocacy seek to influence public policy, laws or budgets, sometimes engaging the media, and nearly always employing message promotion with the aim of informing public office holders and the public in general.

Specific activities of advocacy can include media campaigns, public speaking, and publishing and distributing research.

Lobbying, as a form of advocacy, is a much more direct approach that is made to legislators on a specific issue or specific piece of legislation. Lobbying is far more concentrated and targeted. Lobbying is also legally defined in many jurisdictions – when a form of advocacy has crossed a line and has evolved into an activity subject to laws, rules and regulations - whereas advocacy generally is not.

Types of Advocacy

The three main categories of advocacy are: social advocacy, brand advocacy and political advocacy.

Social advocacy is a practice that focuses on empowerment. Empowering a group of individuals to support your cause or issue entails sharing content and connecting with larger groups of people. The theme of social advocacy relates to social justice, fairness and equity. The activity of "rights movements" (individual rights, civil rights, equal rights) is often found in this type of advocacy.

Brand advocacy focuses on promoting the organization and issue or cause. The process of brand advocacy often relies on "incentivizing", something naturally suited to social media campaigns. The focus here is building affinity, "buy-in", third-party "cheerleaders", so to speak. Efforts here focus on getting people to love your brand, to immediately relate to who you are, and to encouraging them to share that "love" with others.

Political advocacy is the process of advancing change that focuses on government. It is a process that ultimately aims to put an issue on the governing agenda, offering a solution, and building support. And with this type of advocacy one can see that the processes and purposes are not confined to influencing public policy, but also about influencing public opinion.

The three categories are seldom entirely separate from each other, usually overlapping in process and purpose, often inextricably linked.

Regardless of the form or type, advocacy's focal point highlights at least one of the following purposes:

TO INTRODUCE

TO CHANGE

TO OPPOSE

TO ELIMINATE

3

Multiple Professions Use the Terminology

The term "advocacy", as a practice and as a concept, and the term "advocate", as a profession, suggests two distinct paths of speaking on behalf of others; and the distinctions tend to fall into either the legal realm or the political realm. Both legal and political advocates speak for and represent those without a voice.

Both types of advocates help advance causes. And there are several overlapping characteristics between legal and political advocates. For example, both types employ the use of persuasive argument, often backed by various forms of evidence. Herein lies one of the greatest sources of confusion among people who use the term advocacy. So, it's hardly surprising that the definitions are somewhat muddied when, on the one hand, there could be people who desire political or policy change through the contractual retention of an advocate, and, on the other hand, an advocate is strictly a professional who practices in the field of law.

That said, the very same issue could use either type of advocate, though in entirely different ways.

Let's take the issue of physical accessibility for someone using a wheelchair. Let's say that a few friends, each of whom uses a wheelchair for daily mobility, want to make the restrooms in their town's eateries more accessible.

This group could retain the use of an advocate, of the political sort. They want the laws changed so that restrooms are wheelchair accessible. The professional advocate they retain helps create a "campaign", involving media (social and traditional), perhaps a letter-writing exercise targeted to elected officials, perhaps a citizen's support page, as well as the distribution of educational materials (presumably demonstrating how inaccessibility can drive consumer spending dollars to more accessible establishments), and quite often a deputation, presentation or appearance before a legislative or civic committee of government. The result could see the introduction of new legislation, the amendment of existing rules, guidelines or statutes, or the complete elimination from the books of certain laws. The key point in this example highlights the fact that this group wants to achieve greater accessibility by elevating the public, governmental and political attention to the issue of inaccessibility.

Now let's take that very same issue, and say that the same group chooses a legal route (an entirely different process entailing entirely different steps), ultimately having someone speak in court. The public may or may not be aware of the proceedings. Elected officials and other public office holders similarly may be oblivious. In this scenario, the advocate would be focusing arguments on, let's say, the town's building code, or some focal point of civic rights. The advocate in this case is also speaking on behalf of the same group, elevating their issue, but doing so through the legal system, and targeting an outcome that focuses squarely on some existing law, rule or regulation, process or procedure.

Both types, legal and political, entail the use of advocates. Both types can be highly effective in achieving change. Yet, each is a very different creature from the other. The discussion in this book focuses on advocacy that seeks political or policy change. Whereas legal advocates often present in a court of law, serving in a specialist manner, the practice of advocacy favoured in this book rarely, if ever, sees the inside of a courtroom (at least for the purposes of advancing a cause or issue).

Another major source of confusion is found in the practice of lobbying, which is a form of political and policy advocacy. Lobbyists today constitute a profession in many jurisdictions, a profession that is also subject to various reporting and compliance measures imposed by governments. They also seek change by attempting to secure prominence of certain causes or issues on the political and governing agenda. In contrast to many political and policy advocates, who work generally in government and public relations, lobbyists tend to have more specialized expertise, with highly developed relationships and well-honed navigational skills. They know their "stuff" and whose ears to speak to, at any given time. It's not surprising that many lobbyists have advanced their careers from former senior positions in government or political offices (whereas many of today's political advocates may have very little, if any, government or political experience). Another characteristic of lobbyists is that they tend to be more expensive to retain than political advocates (who may or may not be lobbyists).

Incidentally, as we briefly touched upon in Book I, the term lobbyist originates from the word "lobby". There are varying historical explanations. One explanation describes the practice of non-elected officials conducting business with Members of Parliament outside the legislative chamber, in the lobby or waiting room. These individuals gathered in the lobby to influence public officials on legislative matters when those public officials emptied the legislative chamber and filled the lobby. Whether accurate or not, another explanation points to the lobby of the Willard Hotel in Washington, DC, where then-president Ulysses S. Grant would relax with a cigar and brandy – courted by the increasing number of power brokers attracted by that special opportunity to present ideas or advance issues.

Whatever the source, governments around the world today have codes of practice, professional conduct and compliance measures that help define the world of lobbying and the composition of a lobbyist, as opposed to someone who more generally works in advocacy.

Some Key Characteristics

Whether a more generalized advisor on government affairs, or a highly specialized lobbyist, both are advocates who do many things in common with each other:

- They question the way policy is administered;
- They participate in agenda-setting as they raise significant issues;
- They target political systems in response to the needs of individuals or groups;
- They engage a broad range of participants in advancing discussion;
- They propose policy solutions or alternatives; and
- They facilitate a forum or space for public discourse and argumentation.

There are also several common trajectories and targets of advocacy. Government budgets offer a path for committed financial resources and government expenditures (tax-related or otherwise). Bureaucratic advocacy works through systems of consultation as regards specific regulations. Issue advocacy involves considerable effort in public education, and frequently relies on methods associated with public or media affairs. Ideological advocacy is one of the more diffuse forms of advocacy, in that this usually involves groups employing public protests and demonstrations to advance their ideas. Legislative advocacy relies more than anything on the processes through the provincial, state, territorial or federal governments, which typically include committee hearings, presentations and deputations, as part of a strategy to create change. Mass advocacy takes shape through action taken by large groups (via petitions or demonstrations, for example). Media advocacy is usually the strategic use of mass media to advance a social or public policy initiative.

Additionally, any one of these trajectories or targets of advocacy can also (and sometimes necessarily so) focus on advancing brand advocacy – which revolves around the organization behind or promoting the message, which is often critical to the success of advancing any issue or cause.

At its core, regardless of the form, category or type, advocacy is about actively advancing a dialogue through persuasion, and the harnessing of the authority and influence driving that persuasion. Or, put somewhat differently, advocacy is about "selling" and achieving a "buy-in".

4

Contrary to the stigmatized version of a corrupt power broker lurking in dark alleys with payoffs and bribes, lobbyists – indeed all advocates – facilitate the process in which groups can articulate their interests, causes or issues, and ultimately influence public policy and government decision-making. Of course, not everyone will agree with every issue or cause being advanced; however, the lack of consensus on what constitutes interests or issues that are deemed important does not minimize the significance of the process of getting those interests and issues to the table in the first place.

Government decision-making and public policy is a specialized process with a technical outcome. Despite this, governments do not have all the necessary expertise to produce policy outcomes that work well in every region and under every circumstance. The process of advancing issues and causes helps create more effective and more sustainable policy outcomes.

Citizens and groups also use this process to help influence change or to propose alternative solutions. It can be fairly said that efforts to advance the vote for women, or efforts to remove lead from household paint, or measures designed to eliminate drunk driving, for example, are the result of advocacy efforts. Most individuals or groups do not have political or governmental experience, so the use of skilled advocacy representatives and lobbyists can often help that process of influencing change or proposing solutions

Advocacy is an expression of participatory democracy. Conceptually, lobbying is no different.

However, the downside (if there is one) is the institutionalization of lobbying as an industry. As Lee Drutman, in a special to *The Atlantic*, wrote in 2015, "To get corporations to invest fully in politics, lobbyists had to convince companies that Washington could be a profit center. They had to convince them that lobbying was not just about keeping the government far away - it could also be about drawing government close... Today, the biggest companies have upwards of 100 lobbyists representing them, allowing them to be everywhere, all the time." (See Drutman, *The Atlantic*)

While Drutman's estimation seems ominous, Peter Geller, in an article published in *Forbes* (January 2021), has a counterpoint: "Many elected members of Congress appreciate the perspective of their constituents and do not have an intricate understanding of any issue. They are generalists and oftentimes rely on lobbyists for educating on the issues."

A prominent Canadian scholar of public policy, Donald Savoie, offers a differing opinion in a 2019 special to the *Globe and Mail*: "Dennis Mills, a former MP and businessperson who regularly meets with chief executives, summed things up well: 'CEOs no longer know who their MPs are, but they sure know who their lobbyists are,' he told me the other week," writes Savoie. He continues: "It only takes a moment's reflection to appreciate that Canadians cannot afford lobbyists to roam the corridors of power in Ottawa on their behalf. Therein lies the problem. Their MPs are not allowed in to be an effective advocate for the communities they represent or hold the government to account."

So, the practice of lobbying, and what it represents today, is also a reflection on the political process, as well as the efficacy and expertise of the bureaucracy. The impact of various forms of advocacy, particularly paid lobbying of the corporate type, is undeniable. The importance of advocacy, especially as an expression of participatory democracy, is a topic that deserves more attention.

Acknowledgement and Systemization

Governments in multiple jurisdictions have recognized and acknowledged the importance and significance of political advocacy, particularly lobbying, by creating lobbyist registers. Many governments now require anyone defined as a lobbyist to register themselves, their clients, and various activities. The purpose in establishing such registries was to create transparency in the larger system of influencing public policy and government decision-making.

One can be defined as working "in-house" or as a "paid consultant" (external to the organization). Many definitions tend to get a little muddy after that. One quirk in the definitions that many in the profession (as well as many critics) point out is the "time threshold", how activity is quantified. Most legislation around lobbying registration only requires that a person or company register (and later report various activities) provided that a certain number of hours each day, and averaged every month, are routinely dedicated to "lobbying" activity. Furthermore, "lobbying" excludes a range of activity (many definitions do not count public consultations as part of lobbying). A single phone call from a bank CEO to the Minister of Finance, during a pre-budget work-up, is not typically defined as lobbying. So, while lobbying has been formally acknowledged as a legitimate part of the policy and legislative systems of many jurisdictions, the multiple exemptions written into the legislative definitions contribute to "grey zones" and the shift to using other terms that describe one's advocacy work (such as government relations or government affairs specialists). These are nuances and quirks that can be addressed and improved, a topic that is addressed in later discussions that highlight the preponderance of legislators to focus their regulatory efforts disproportionately on corporate lobbyists (as opposed to a more broad-based application to advocacy professionals in general).

The fact is that governments have not banned lobbying, but instead recognized the practice and formalized (perhaps even institutionalized) it into the public policy and decision-making process.

Most organizations today have some form of an advocate. Some organizations, both for-profit and non-profit, appoint a government specialist to their board (or a committee of the corporation). Others hire generalists with experience in the political, governmental or public affairs fields. Others are more fully committed, with individuals (internal or external) and entire departments or units whose performance is measured by influencing the political and policy agenda as per the mission and priorities of their company (for-profit, non-profit or charitable). Like most other commodities on the market, the higher the quality, and the higher the chance of achieving defined deliverables (that is, policy or agenda influence), the higher the price. Advocates who focus on full-time lobbying, as opposed to nurturing relationships, usually demand significantly higher prices.

5

There are four major approaches in the world of advocacy. A common approach to advancing a cause or issue is to attempt to elevate awareness during an electoral campaign, often with the aim of influencing the position of political parties or candidates. Another approach that is likely familiar to most people is the "mass" or "public" route, which relies heavily on demonstrations, protests and assemblies. A less publicly visible approach works more methodically, exploiting formal opportunities for consultation, feedback and input in the public policy process. Finally, the least publicly visible approach seeks change by directly engaging targeted public office holders and decision makers. The reality for most advocacy efforts in practice takes shape as a blend of at least two approaches. The exact mix of approaches, and the selection of specific methods and techniques, depends on several considerations, which are described shortly. But first, let's look at the textbook, standard steps and methods in advocacy.

Typical Planning Methodology

The "textbook" steps in advocacy have been pushed *ad infinitum* by a spectrum of educators and trainers. Whether running advocacy workshops (many use the word "lobby workshops" despite its questionable applicability) that may be coordinated by your industry association, trade union, or other organization, or studying advocacy methods in a university or college course, many people's experience tends to echo the "textbook" steps (all of which are useful, despite the fact that they are seldom used in practice in such a formulaic way).

1. Set your Goal

As part of establishing that ultimate target, most conventional advice recommends the following:

- Specificity: Be specific about what you want to accomplish with your advocacy campaign;
- Measurability: Quantify your goal, which facilitates the tracking of progress and the confirmation of subsequent steps;
- Attainability: Focus on deliverables and what is do-able;
- Relevance: Define how the goal, and the objectives of that goal, will produce benefits (and to whom); and
- Timeliness: Deadlines also help define goals. Even ongoing advocacy will have points of achievement, and, quite often, beginnings and ends.

2. Identify your Target

Prior to any efforts designed to change policies or laws, it is vital to identify the people who are in a position to make that change. This is the target of your advocacy.

3. Build Your Team

Nearly every advocacy initiative or project requires more than one person. Advocacy teams include administration, content creation and promotion, sponsors, and volunteer/network/community engagement.

4. Define Your Message

Focus on crafting your messaging, which will be used to engage supporters and ultimately reach the campaign target. Part of defining the message is correctly defining the problem - the other key part of appreciating how a chosen solution relates to the problem.

5. Map a Timeline

Mapping requires realistic, not idealistic, considerations. Identify and factor-in internal and external considerations.

These textbook steps can be a useful starting point. They represent the routinized, formulaic steps found in most textbooks that discuss advocacy, activism and civic engagement. The reality is more muddied, conceptual, creative and nuanced to a given project.

What Do You Hope to Achieve?

This is the critical question that needs to be addressed prior to engaging in any advocacy. It's a question that should also be asked sporadically throughout the advocacy process. Inextricably connected to this question is deciding whether the efforts are singular and one-off in execution, or if the efforts are ongoing and must be systematized into the operations of an organization.

Most advocacy work is geared to shaping public policy, in some form and at some point. A singular and one-off effort can consume many months, and sometimes years, especially if, for example, the type of policy change targeted involves taxation; alternatively, with some careful planning, some one-off efforts are complete in a relatively short period of time, especially those that respond to a government consultation or other form of solicitation by public office holders. Either way, the group executing the advocacy has only a single goal (relatively speaking). Once achieved (measures of performance are discussed later), the advocacy campaign wraps up. In contrast, ongoing efforts often involve nurturing long-term relationships, and such ongoing work is an expression of the degree to which the organization's operations and mission are tied to government decision-making and government activity in general, as well as those that are heavily regulated by government measures (such as air transport and pharmaceutical firms).

So, identifying and understanding what your organization wants to achieve, and whether that goal is a one-off exercise or something ongoing and continual, represent the first step: moving from a broader conceptualization of needing advocacy to being in a position suitable to identifying methods and techniques that will influence the desired target of public policy.

Know Your Issue

For some, outside expertise is recruited during the process of defining goals and objectives. For most, that expertise is typically sought during the process of defining and knowing the issue (a process that ought to proceed the definition of goals and objectives, but usually this is not the case; most organizations tend to assume a level of knowledge of the issue at hand – until they realize that they don't understand and appreciate the issue from a holistic perspective as would be the case for an external, objective advisor). Knowing the issue can actually consume more time than many people realize, as this step defines the trajectory of nearly every other action thereafter.

As explained in Book I, *Content Creation and Promotion*, knowing a problem is harder than it seems. The main reason for this is that too many people are not effective listeners. It's only through attentive listening that we can correctly identify and define a problem, which can then help create a foundation for a potential solution. Don't fall in love with the solution; there are already too many solutions for every problem that exists. Instead, fall in love with the problem, savour the problem, learn to know it and understand it. With that knowledge, you will have the prerequisites of influence and authority.

What are the Legal and Ethical Considerations?

In proceeding with any advocacy (whether legally defined as lobbying or not), diarize all activities related to the efforts. Keep a record of meetings, topics of discussion, places and amounts of any expenses incurred, for any internal or external reporting, existing or potential. Having this information at the beginning makes things so much easier should a formal lobbying registration become necessary. Even if this is not the case, record-keeping should be a matter of course for any organization or individual. In all forms of advocacy, transparency and accountability to members, directors or other key stakeholders - including those related to government compliance – must be a natural part of the process of attempting to shape public policy.

Are there any other issues that may impact the reputation of the organization by endorsing or promoting an issue or cause? For example, it has become commonplace for corporate positioning to align with social causes and issues (from financial institutions sponsoring Pride events to sponsors withdrawing their corporate support for a given activity in an effort to persuade social change). Are these endeavours in advocacy consistent with the mission and objectives of the organization, of its membership principles and donors? Alternatively, is moving in a bold, uncharted advocacy trajectory something that demonstrates leadership and potentially even greater respect for the organization?

The legal and ethical considerations, which can affect brand reputation, need to be flushed out early in the process.

Know the Landscape of Governance

Whether the issue or cause at hand is new and innovative, one that responds to an existing government policy or process, or one that seeks to eliminate a regulation or rule, it is critical to know the landscape of governance. Within this landscape are the entities that develop and administer the legislation, policies and processes, and rules and regulations of your issue.

This landscape includes many entities: legislatures (municipal, indigenous, territorial, provincial, state and federal); the officers of that legislature (which typically are the elected representatives); the departments and ministries in the bureaucracy or public service; the leader's office (the entity that houses and supports the chief, mayor, premier, governor, etc.); arms-length agencies, boards and commissions; other para-public entities (such as educational institutions, police, health and military organizations); and, depending on the issue, international agencies and collaborations. Knowing how a "bill becomes a law" is certainly useful (the 1970s educational cartoon about this topic, widely available on YouTube, and likely embedded in the memories of many people as a useful reference). This is the critical navigational know-how; having that know-how is essential to understanding the flow and centre of authority, influence and power in the governing system in question.

Knowing this landscape as it pertains to your issue or cause is vital to correctly navigating a suitable path of advocacy.

From Introspection to Outreach

Defining goals and objectives, as well as defining and savouring the problem, represent processes that are highly introspective. These processes many yield some surprising answers about the organization, about the issue or cause it seeks to promote, or about the product, service or system/group it represents; and the answers can often help position one's advocacy efforts more synchronously with the public policy systems at which those efforts will ultimately be aimed.

From these processes of introspection, the focus turns to tactics, strategy and outreach.

At the early stages in "practical matters", one-off or singular efforts closely resemble those of the ongoing and systematized sort. The external consultant and the internal advocacy professional resemble each other at this early stage. Interestingly, even one-off and singular advocacy efforts can seem like an ongoing process.

Whether the organization decides to formalize an advocacy position or unit within its operations, or an external "lobbying" group is retained, the preliminary stages are similar: both must focus on the need to package the message and reach out to the appropriate audience. So what are the methods and techniques of outreach?

Developing Awareness and Building Affinity with Supporters

A common first step in advocacy is building awareness. Every organization has a network, community of supporters, constituency, clientele, or consumer base of some sort. The first step is to solidify this community, thus reinforcing brand, and ideally building a stronger affinity to the organization and its mission.

It really doesn't matter what the issue is. It doesn't matter if you're proposing a new innovation or government regulation, recommending the alteration of an existing rule, or working to eliminate something altogether.

The first step is to communicate this information to those already in your realm of capture. This can be done through a variety of means: any social media that allows "posting", facilitates "shares", and elicits "likes"; podcasts and related audio media forums; YouTube and related video media forums; a dedicated Reddit subgroup, with regular posting and engagement in related subreddits; direct mail and email; and a designated place on your organization's website (or a new, but integrated, website). This community of interested and supporting individuals are your organization's potential fan base and "cheerleaders". When properly engaged, they will help promote further awareness through their own outreach.

This community is your organization's family, so treat them as such. Communicate regularly and conversationally. Every now and then consider quoting that one individual who made a constructive comment on social media, for example. Acknowledge and thank contributors to online forums and discussions.

Routinely, but sparingly, reference parts of your organization's mission, objective and goals with something like "after all, our core values have always stood for …" This effort can help remind people what the organization is all about. Always include a link to an online page where you host your base "about" message (regardless of where you have decided that page should reside). This page (or website) should also include background and referential material, cases, interesting facts, downloadable images and statistical information, etc.

Finally, consider how your community can get involved, how you can further engage them. Sometimes basic and clear instructions that "connect the dots" are what people want. In addition to the educational materials, which help people to "learn more" about the issue and those behind it, provide plenty of suggestions on what people can do. These suggestions could be simple steps, such as asking people to share the online information with three individuals via email, or adding a reference of your organization's website to their own websites. Perhaps one or two people want to produce TikTok videos demonstrating how your organization (and, ideally, the issue you're promoting) is important to them. Others might dedicate one or two episodes of their own podcasts to talking about and interviewing organization representatives, which helps advance the issue to their listeners. The older methods of advocacy used at this stage often employed the "tool kit" approach. The "tool kit", usually available as a dedicated webpage, provided samples (that simply required the insertion of specific names and addresses): letters to the editor; letters to elected representatives; or questions that could be posed to public office holders or candidates for office at a local town-hall meeting. An even older approach, but one that can attract a certain amount of attention, is old-fashioned letter-writing, using pen, paper, envelope and a stamp. Engaging your community to send hard-copy mail about your organization or issue has a considerably different impact than sending email: hard-copy mail is physical and difficult to eliminate by pressing a button, and accordingly commands a different quality of attention.

Again, these steps not only help develop affinity and reinforce your organization's community base, the outreach and engagement involved also assist in reinforcing the organization's reputation.

Building and Nurturing Relations in the Landscape of Governance

As implied in this sub-heading, this is an inherently methodical (and sometimes slower) process. It takes time to build anything, and, in the case of advocacy, both the process of building and the process of nurturing are ongoing.

A new organization, or an existing organization with a newly instituted advocacy/government relations unit, must first identify every point-person in every department, ministry, agency, board or commission that somehow touches the cause or issue at hand. Surprising to many people, this footprint in the landscape of governance is often much larger than expected.

Let's consider the issue of homelessness. The footprint in the landscape of governance for homelessness is expansive. To begin with, one needs to consider the levels of government involved in homelessness within the region or jurisdiction at hand (quite often, different levels of government work collaboratively in matters such as homelessness). Within each level of government there are several other possible points of relevance: realty, land use and property development; residential zoning issues; urban issues; family, women and children's issues; seniors; the overall income tax structure; poverty reduction initiatives; community development; employment; immigration; social and traditional media of relevance; other organizations advocating similar or related issues to homelessness; and health and healthcare, to name a few. Beyond the entities of governance other potential parties could include academic and research institutes focused on the above-referenced topics; related professional associations; and, of course, those with the lived experience themselves. So, even an issue described with a single word can have a surprisingly large footprint in the landscape of governance.

The Realm of Capture

How does all this relate to putting advocacy into practice? After identifying the players in the landscape, the new advocacy initiative needs to "capture" its landscape. Capturing involves both establishing a two-way process of communication as well as forging a reputation of reliable expertise and opinion. Central in this process is reciprocity, providing people with something useful.

The knee-jerk reaction by many people to promoting an issue or cause is to simply ask for something, such as tax expenditures or additional funding. Seldom are things so simple. Homelessness, for example, illustrates the multi-dimensionality that often defines any given issue.

Introductory outreach is valuable for any advocacy initiative in this stage. It is essential to communicate with key point-people in each of the units of relevance. Let them know that you exist, what you have to offer, and why you consider your issue important. Let them know that you're available to collaborate. Most importantly, provide something of value. This could be as simple as sharing the results of a study, related news stories, perhaps internal organizational updates or snippets from an annual report.

Regular communication of the sort described above needs to follow introductory outreach. And the more useful and valued your communication is viewed, the more important you and your organization become. The point is to not only have a proverbial "seat at the table", but to be perceived as having one.

But this takes time. Remember, this is an ongoing process of constantly identifying, building and nurturing.

Even at this early stage, multiple forms of advocacy are in play, notably issue advocacy, bureaucratic advocacy and brand advocacy. By reaching out, and building relationships with key point-people in the landscape of governance, advocacy efforts promote and reinforce the brand of your organization as well as the issue you hold dear.

Points of Influence

Consultations with government and its organizations in the para-public sector represent highly useful points of influence. Government departments, agencies, boards and commissions routinely solicit opinion and feedback on proposed policy and legislative measures. Some consultations are impersonal, and entail the completion of an online survey, for example, or the submission of a response with recommendations. Other consultations take shape as town-hall forums or roundtables of representatives. A common approach in consultations is the use of public/committee hearings, and the accompanying practice of receiving expert testimony, presentations, and deputations to committees of legislators.

Use all points of influence in this regard, sharing your organization's opinions and expertise in as many points of influence in the landscape of governance. This not only helps broaden the audience for your organization's advocacy efforts, it also helps expand your field of capture. Consider consultations that are both directly and indirectly related.

Incidentally, your organization's efforts in advancing dialogue on a given issue or cause will also end up reinforcing the importance and significance of the "public" in public policy. The ongoing process of building and nurturing represents a type of "soft" advocacy that shares, informs, and assists representatives and lawmakers.

Mentioned earlier was the use of the electoral cycle, and how some advocacy efforts target political parties and candidates during an election campaign. The evidence on the effectiveness and efficacy of this approach is mixed. That said, a version of this approach, one that is seldom used, can be deliver effective results: targeting constituency and legislative offices of elected officials between electoral periods.

Constituency and legislative offices, and the all-important staff that run them, offer unique points of influence – provided the outreach to these point-people is considered useful and informative. One "mini" advocacy effort that I oversaw one summer consisted of outreach (in-person, email and physical mail) to every legislative and constituency office of the provincial elected officials in Ontario. The effort was conducted during the summer months, typically a time when the elected official is not present as regularly in those settings. But the staffs in both types of office were considered vital, with high levels of expertise and unique positions of influence in their respective spheres. Our efforts targeted the staffs, not the elected officials. Our message - which emanated from an organization that provided services to people with disabilities – focused on seven simple ways to make their offices more accessible for anyone with a disability. And the format was a simple postcard, the front of which extended "Seasons' Greetings" (a summertime play on the December holiday card, which, although somewhat gimmicky, generated considerable attention), with the reverse of the card highlighting the key points, the organization's logo, and contact information. The advocacy project was aimed at a key group; it was designed to capture attention, and it was delivered with information considered useful by the recipient. It's a promotional tool and a technique that is certainly not new (real estate agents have been distributing fridge magnets and calendars for many years); but it's an approach that is frequently overlooked in the world of advocacy, notably during the ongoing process of building and nurturing relations in the landscape of governance.

In addition to government committees, studies and roundtables, the budgetary process is a key point of influence. Most governments today hold some version of a pre-budget consultation, a process whereby governments reach out to sectoral representatives for the purpose of soliciting recommendations on spending priorities.

Any communication with an official committee, roundtable or other similar consultation by government represents an opportunity to get into the official and permanent legislative record. While most people unfamiliar with government records of proceedings likely will not see much value in such an achievement, people in the landscape of governance certainly do: it helps develop cache and reputation. Again, such an effort also advances brand advocacy, as it elevates profile while simultaneously advancing an issue or cause.

Bottom line: get on the record as much as possible

Statements by representatives in a legislature also represent a method of getting on the legislative record. A "statement" consists of a brief paragraph, delivered aloud by the elected official in the legislature, and highlights the importance of a cause, organization, event or some other item of importance. Such "statements" contribute to issue awareness as well as brand awareness, as the transcript and video record can then be repackaged and repurposed - distributed to the organization's realm of capture (that network of supporters discussed earlier), who then have a tangible tool to help further advance the organization's cause, thus becoming a "cheerleader".

Events can often represent points of influence. Whether in-person or through virtual conferencing, receptions and town-halls concentrate interested individuals, share information, help expand communication, reinforce networks, and advance advocacy efforts in general.

Another method sometimes used is collaboration with a champion. Champions are those individuals you can comfortably identify as a supporter. For example, collaboration with a Senator, Member of Parliament, or Representative might take the form of a co-written article for publication in a political or policy journal. The legislative districts in Ottawa and Washington, DC, for example, both have political/policy trade publications that are considered "must-reads". Discovering your champions, and collaborating in mutually beneficial ways, can sometimes produce results with a surprisingly long shelf-life.

Media is another point of influence, though one that is far less concentrated than others in the landscape of governance. Panel shows or paid advertisements can reach large numbers of people. At the very least, such methods are valuable in helping expand and reinforce both issue advocacy and brand advocacy.

Podcasts and video content, self-produced or otherwise, each have their own benefits, a topic that is flushed out in other sections of this book. For now, suffice to say that both vehicles can potentially impact larger numbers of people and quite often in more measurable ways.

The final method discussed here is the use of allies and partners, all those "others" in or connected to your organization's realm of capture, for possible coalitions and alliances. Coalitions and alliances are explored in a dedicated, later chapter, as this method has significant advantages and disadvantages.

Reflection and Recap

The advocacy professional needs to find the most effective ways to exert influence on a political or policy agenda.

Sometimes advocacy professionals will "lobby" one another. There are instances in which normally opposing groups find a common area of interest, and this common area can serve as a foundation for a united front.

If the advocacy takes the form of lobbying, the methods and techniques can be quite direct and explicit. This type of advocacy typically takes shape as a meeting with elected representatives and public officer holders, and providing them with information pertinent to a bill (commonly used in corporate lobbying).

Sometimes, advocacy professionals will work with a politician or an elected representative in drafting legislation that is mutually beneficial. This role exemplifies the link between communication and public policy.

Social outreach can be a critical method of advocating. Some professionals engage in social outreach, like hosting receptions, which facilitate interaction among the various stakeholders and decision makers in a less formal, but highly informative, atmosphere.

Advocacy is also prevalent at the grassroots level. This form of advocacy is also known as indirect lobbying, or grassroots lobbying. For example, grassrooters enlist the help of the community to influence candidates or elected representatives by writing, calling, mobilizing online, demonstrating on the organization's behalf, serving as content creators (for example, writing and posting articles for traditional and social media), or assisting in media outreach and liaison (for example, securing participation in on-air talk shows, podcasts or YouTube videos as a means to generating interest in and awareness of their issues).

It shouldn't be surprising that many advocacy professionals, particularly those who fall within the definitions of lobbyists, have previous careers in the political and governmental worlds. Many formally served as legislators, appointed bureaucrats or political aides. As such, they are able to capitalize on their years of experience and the interconnected networks generated by that experience (referred to as the "revolving door", a practice that legislation now regulates in some jurisdictions).

The Most Effective Technique in Advocacy: Don't Raise Your Voice; Improve Your Argument

This bit of advice referenced in the above subheading is actually a quote attributed to the South African cleric, the late Desmond Tutu, a man who was honored with the Nobel Peace Prize for his opposition to apartheid in South Africa. He was an activist. He was a mobilizer. He was an influencer. He was also wise enough to know that "raising the volume" alone is associated more with cheap gimmicks than it is with achieving sustainable policy change.

Volume is needed. There are times when, without public awareness and "buy-in", the likelihood of change is limited. In today's world of ever-shorter bursts of information, loud and cheap attention-getting gimmicks are increasingly popular in the world of advancing issues. While there is a place for such "louder" methods, it is a place that should be approached sparingly, complemented by caution and substantive measures that speak to policy change as an outcome instead of street theatre or social media bursts as a means.

6

Advocacy requires a pause every now and then, a reflection, and the careful consideration of several questions: Are we moving in the right direction? How do we know? How do we describe the milestones in our project? When all is said and done, how do we know if and when we are successful?

These are questions that must be posed during the conceptual and planning stages of formulating an advocacy campaign, and must be asked throughout the campaign itself.

Whether directing the work in-house or externally for a client, defined measures address issues of accountability, such as contract performance and deliverables.

Was Change Achieved?

In the more focused world of legally-defined lobbying, a typical target of the advocacy campaign is a change to legislation in direct response to the advocacy efforts implemented. One of the more obvious indicators of performance in political advocacy is whether or not the target – a piece of legislation - was changed in the organization's or client's favour.

Campaigns like this often necessarily entail multiple trajectories and forms of advocacy, often stretching over more than one legislative session, so it is usually advised to identify smaller steps and individual milestones, as part of the larger change targeted.

Were the Organization's Goals Furthered?

The organization's goals can also be furthered by complementary advocacy work. For example, an advocacy project for a poverty reduction group would likely consider several policy areas of interest, including working with committees dedicated to housing, employment or community development. Contributing to such dialogue also raises awareness of the organization and its work, something most would consider as furthering the goals of an organization. How do we measure increased awareness of the organization and its cause? There are many examples of such metrics: Unsolicited invitations, let's say to participate in a Minister's policy roundtable could indicate broader and increased awareness of the organization. Were the goals furthered? Answering this question requires an understanding that political advocacy entails political conversations; a process that, it could be said, reflects a successful advancement of the dialogue (overall trends and policy directions).

Did the Organization Experience Any Growth as a Result of the Advocacy Campaign?

Even campaigns that don't change legislation still have the potential to help an organization grow their influence and resources. Measures can include increased donations, more supporters or paid members, more volunteers, increased active volunteer engagement, or increased social media activity. Measuring such indicators obviously requires an organization to have the tools and capacity to measure such metrics. A short-term measure of success is not always dependent on targeted legislation.

Challenges of Measurement

While there are some tangible measures of success, evaluating any advocacy campaign can be a challenge. Steven Teles, of Johns Hopkins University, and Mark Schmitt, of the New American Foundation, explain in their article entitled, "The Elusive Craft of Evaluating Advocacy": "Advocacy evaluation should be seen as a form of trained judgment, rather than a method. That judgment requires a deep knowledge of and feel for the politics of the issues, strong networks of trust to the key players, an ability to assess organizational quality, and a sense for the right time horizon against which to measure accomplishments."

Advocacy is a Long Game

Most advocacy campaigns are long-term. Work may span several legislative sessions, often requiring a "re-tooling" should an election occur. Tax issues, in particular, necessarily must account for the processes and timeframes around legislative committees, the introduction of bills, the process of advancing a bill from the legislature, through consultation and further committee deliberations, and back to the legislature. Many other forms of complementary advocacy work can be executed concurrently, and these smaller steps and milestones can contribute to a more refined definition of success. However, advocacy is generally long-term, and even the most seasoned of professionals will sometimes struggle with defining measures and metrics.

Did Your Effort Make the Difference, or Was it Something Else?

One should be so lucky to have their issue or cause identified in an executive order, a Throne Speech or a State of the Union Address. Yet these achievements occasionally happen, where a broader issue related to a specific policy envelope is referenced as a priority in the announcement of a governing agenda.

The challenge for those attempting to measure and evaluate success in this instance is determining if their advocacy efforts were responsible. The advocacy team could list the number of meetings conducted on the issue, the number of presentations made, and the numbers and types of outreach to legislators and related staff. However, to be so bold as to formally attribute such efforts and milestones to something much higher and larger is difficult without firm evidence.

Changing Priorities

If only one example is used to explain the nature of changing priorities, surely the global pandemic caused by COVID-19 should suffice for most readers. There are changing priorities on an ongoing basis, but the pandemic produced a more meaningful "ah, yes, I understand" type of response.

The work and trajectory of an organization's advocacy efforts sometimes need to be adapted, often redefined as regards deliverables and what is actually do-able, as circumstances beyond one's control alter the landscape. Evaluating performance and identifying measures of success when confronting periods of changing priorities can represent a unique challenge for advocacy teams.

What this highlights for planners of advocacy campaigns is the need to focus and define priority issues versus secondary issues. Added to this is the question of knowing what precisely to measure. For example, is outreach a primary concern in the advocacy project? If so, how is that outreach measured: by number of communications via phone or email, or the number of incoming messages or inquiries of interest? Is growth part of the evaluation? In other words, do the performance measures evaluate those numbers from one period compared with another? How long are the intervals between periods? Many advocacy teams employ various social media, and here, too, measurement and definition are instrumental to success: the number of followers; the number of new or previously unaffiliated followers; the number of likes; the number of shares; the number of conversations engaged; the number and amount of donations; or the number of users who explicitly indicate support by digitally signing a petition. Knowing what and how to measure is a significant (and sometimes creative) part of defining success and other metrics in the advocacy journey.

The measures of performance and definitions of success form a large part of the final report of results from the advocacy efforts. They demonstrate exactly what was done to fulfil the details of the contract or performance agreement, whether the work was focused on advancing or elevating, influencing or building, or producing the changes desired in the form of introducing, proposing, changing or eliminating a policy, law or process. Advocacy teams need to engage in revisiting these measures as part of a process of periodic reflection and confirmation of the team's work, its impact, and the expectations from clients or other parts of the team's organization.

7

There are several types of organizational structures when two or more groups choose to work collaboratively towards a common goal: partnerships, collaborations, alliances or allegiances, and coalitions. While similar, the differences in each depends on the degree of relative autonomy of the key actors, how those actors structurally address operational matters, and the longevity of the project at hand. It's interesting how the words - coalition, alliance, partnership, collaboration - are used interchangeably by professionals and organizational representatives engaged in the practice of advocacy.

Collaborations, alliances and allegiances suggest a greater degree of relative autonomy of each actor. This occurs when two or more parties endorse the same goal, and usually suggests coordinated activity aimed at achieving that goal. These structures can last as long as the respective leadership in each group deems suitable.

A coalition is a group of like-minded organizations or individuals who unite to create policy change. Coalitions usually imply coordinated activity on a structural level. For example, three organizations working towards the introduction of a new tax credit might create a steering committee composed of relevant operational representatives from each organization, who then report to each other and share experience and information. The coalition almost always suggests an added component of administration that centralizes operations, much like the centre of the spokes on a wheel. Given the resource commitments of each actor, coalitions tend to be more time-bound to the issue at hand.

A partnership represents a joining and unification of forces. Partnerships can emerge as entirely new structures, with dedicated staff and operational mandates. Partnerships can also appear as a merger between two previously separate organizations. Partnerships tend to focus on broader concepts, such as advancing the health and growth of the banking sector, greater participation of seniors in society, or promoting awareness and best practices for healthy lifestyles for children. Partnerships tend to be ongoing or indefinite.

Without a doubt, the knee-jerk reaction to advancing an issue or cause collectively is to recommend the formation of a coalition. Advocacy coalitions (whether appropriately named or not) represent a particularly popular go-to option for individuals and organizations in the non-profit and charitable sectors.

Regardless of how they are named or how they operate, each of these structures and approaches to advocacy is an association. Historically, associations have shown promising potential to influence public policy. However, experience also tells us that, unless structured as a partnership, most associations (especially those designed as coalitions) tend to be temporary.

Why is Working with Another Organization Important?

Advocacy and government relations efforts are time-consuming, costly and demand a considerable level of expertise. It is a rare instance, indeed, to find sufficient resources for all issues within a given organization, especially those working in the non-profit or charitable sectors (where salaries tend to be lower and less competitive with the private sector). Even those in the corporate/private sector world might not possess all the necessary expertise needed in every instance. In other words, most organizations have a resource deficit of some sort. Associations can represent a practical response to such deficits.

Associations can be well-suited to broadening the base of support for a particular position by leveraging their infrastructure and realm of capture (or operational eco-system). Effective associations, particularly if managed as a coalition, suggest a number of benefits to members and supporters, such as more effective networking and exchange of information, increased access to resources, efficiency of accountability, and improved problem-solving.

Possible Drawbacks to the Coalition

The biggest drawback to a coalition echoes a recurring theme in this Book: time. On the one hand, advocacy takes time in order to achieve policy change. Yet, on the other hand, many advocacy coalitions are temporal in nature (sometimes due to limited resources, even as a collective association), and the members of which do not appreciate the longevity of the work. Advocacy is a journey, and rarely a quick-fix. A lack of understanding and appreciation among the coalition members can represent a serious drawback in choosing to form an association in the first place. This leads us to the second biggest drawback, one that touches on the subject of cohesiveness.

Cohesiveness is difficult enough to achieve within one organization; the difficulty is enhanced as other organizations structurally work in coalition with each other. One of the biggest drawbacks in any coalition can be found in the conflicts that can arise due to lack of understanding (or misunderstanding) about the other partners in the group and how their organizations operate.

Power, both real and perceived, is another common source of conflict within a coalition. Politics is about power; advocacy and government relations seek to influence the decisions and choices in that realm. Who has greater authority and influence (again, real or perceived) can determine whether or not a power struggle is likely to emerge.

When is a Coalition Useful?

An interesting way to address this question recalls the definition of an advocacy coalition by political scientist, Leslie Pal, who describes an advocacy coalition as follows: "a wide range of actors, including government from all levels, officials, interest organizations, research groups, journalists, and even other countries, who share a belief system about a policy area, and over time demonstrate some degree of coordinated activities." (See Pal, *Beyond Policy Analysis*)

An advocacy coalition is particularly useful when the intended policy change entails a new area or proposal in public policy, as well as when attempting to persuade decision makers of a certain level of budget allocation for a specific program or issue – in other words, things that are new and things that cost money.

The expression that equates greater strength with higher numbers is instrumental in this regard. In practice, one shows the breadth and depth of support. The usefulness of any advocacy coalition increases when broader "buy-in" or support must be demonstrated. Some methods of persuasion must go beyond an exercise of outlining the technical benefits, and demonstrate how the proposals for policy change not only reflect a broader belief system in society, but are also resonant with the belief systems existing in the landscape of governance.

Steps in Creating the Association

Regardless of the type of association one chooses, action proceeds from the recognition that somehow working with other stakeholders is useful, perhaps even necessary.

Identify and Reach Out

The first step is to identify appropriate partners who, in the first instance, may have complementary and competing positions in an organization's sector or realm of capture. Other attributes, such as organizational skills, financial resources, experience and spheres of influence, will certainly play a part. Once identified, pick up the phone. Of course, accompanying that step in outreach is a clear and well-understood position on the issue as well as the benefits of association. Potential partners must be solicited, with a similar degree of definition and clarity as one would find in a corporate prospectus.

Establish Mutual Principles and Practices

In addition to the mission, goal and objectives of the coalition, roles and resources must be outlined. Budgets and work plans must be designed. Leadership and spokespeople must be identified. Operational meetings need to be scheduled.

Internal flows of communication must be established. And external messaging – including branding – will be essential to any type of advocacy association.

Identify Milestones and Points of Influence

Most advocacy efforts are long-term initiatives. Within those timelines of work there will be points of influence, or opportunities to participate, thus broadening organizational profile, encouraging supporters, maximizing opportunities for engagement, and possibly securing additional resources. For example, consider participating in individual yet related (even if indirectly) committee presentations, or participation in any of the multiple points of entry in the budgetary process.

As part of this process, it is critical to identify those members and staff who can best influence the decision-making process for the specific issue at hand (for example, media, elected officials, other public office holders, local/community political groups, etc.)

Keys to Success

Political scientist, Paul Sabatier, wrote in 1993 that successful advocacy coalitions have many characteristics, but four of them tend to stand out:

1. Members understand that the policy change requires time (sometimes more than a decade, depending on the issue);

2. Members appreciate that it is beneficial and practical to logistically break-down the longer timespans into "policy subsystems";

3. Members appreciate the intergovernmental and intersectionality of most areas of public policy (that is, nothing operates in a vacuum from other policy areas, and most areas entail or affect different levels or realms of governance); and

4. Members understand that public policy areas (or spheres), and their tangible manifestation - programs - are analogous to belief systems, systems that prioritize and compartmentalize ideas and views about the world. (See Sabatier, "Policy Change Over a Decade")

If participants in an advocacy coalition appreciate these traits of public policy and policy change, the coalition will likely have the perquisites to tackle the technical and instrumental decisions needed to influence the "policy core", a place where decisions are made on issues such as administrative rules, budgetary allocations, and statutory interpretation.

8

Earlier we referenced the use of petitions as a form of advocating for a cause. Petitions are quite popular with some people. While a roster of signatures and endorsements can represent an impressive breadth and depth of support, lists of names do not mean that petitions are useful in and of themselves. In other words, there isn't a single solution to achieving advocacy goals.

Similarly, just because a method worked before shouldn't lead one to believe that it will necessarily work again. Advocacy campaigns have evolved over the years, meaning the trends of successful advocacy campaigns today may not match up with the trends and lessons from even five years ago.

As quickly as something can go "viral" through a social media platform or series of networks, the demographics of those platforms can also change with amazing velocity. The platforms, networks and demographics should not be considered static. As was pointed out in Books I and II, what worked last year, on a specific platform, using a given set of methods and outreach, won't necessarily deliver the success hoped for when executed at a different time.

In addition to correctly conceptualizing and defining the problem at hand (which was more fully explored in Book I), it is equally important to consider the user demographics within the geography you hope to mobilize. These are key considerations for online and digital innovations. Keep abreast of the changing landscape, and keep informed.

Another general consideration to keep in mind is that new innovations should not be viewed as replacing older, more traditional approaches; indeed, quite often it is possible to combine both, with each complementing the other. Again, referencing the discussion from

Book I, I'm reminded of a lecture I once gave to a university class studying advocacy methods for various political and social causes. I encouraged these young women and men to embrace, but to not rely exclusively on, digital media simply because it's fast, newer or easy. Anyone can sign her or his name to an electronic petition as easily as pressing a button. There is really not much engagement or thought happening in the process. And the problem increasingly is that legislators are aware of this fact, which is why e-petitions can have limited effectiveness. Your representative in Congress, or your Member of Parliament, knows that your electronic petition, despite its volume of digital signatures, has limited authority. Older approaches, in contrast, can make a different impact. For example, two mail bags filled with letters or postcards, let's say, each hand-written and signed, represent considerably more effort, thought and authority. Much like the closing court scene in the film, *A Miracle of 34th Street*, when bags and bags of Post Office letters are presented to the judge, carefully choose the most suitable medium to parlay your message. Do it right, and you'll be in a better position to make a lasting impact.

Digital Methods, Tools and Benefits

Today, even the smallest, most grassroots of campaigns employ software and digital innovations for messaging, outreach, recruitment and engagement.

Online Meetings, Conferences, Receptions and Information Sessions

Virtual events have increasingly become the norm. Digital meetings, using Teams or Zoom (and there are many more applications), are highly cost-effective organizational tools that readily facilitate interaction and engagement.

Entire conferences, receptions, Q&A sessions and town-halls are now hosted online. Since 2020, the use of virtual meeting rooms has been embraced by legislatures at all levels worldwide. Put simply, if legislators can meet virtually to vote on a law, then the use of the same digital meeting tools apply just as suitably to the world of advocacy and government relations.

Nothing will ever completely replace the benefits and qualities of an in-person meeting:

the nuances of body language; the tactile feel of a new product or demonstration model; or the simple handshake. And this is where the quality of the "old" and the cost-effectiveness of the "new" can work in complementary ways.

Peer-to-Peer Campaigns

Digital and online outreach can be perfectly suited for peer-to-peer advocacy. Peer-to-peer advocacy taps into, leverages, and aims to mobilize the networks of your supporters. These networks can include family, friends, and colleagues.

Distributing your advocacy message, and recruiting supporters, is sometimes more effective when facilitated through the recommendation of a close and trusted contact. The question employed is usually something to the effect of "Do you know three people whom you trust, and that you can ask for support?" Social media and communication outreach (through email, for example) are highly effective vehicles for peer-to-peer approaches.

Personalized Messaging

Digital outreach has made it possible to connect supporters, members, donors, public office holders and elected officials at virtually any time, from virtually anywhere. As was pointed out earlier, many people, legislators and public office holders included, have grown wise to broad-based, generic online marketing. Translation: personal stories, and that personal "touch", are more important than ever. It is critical to an advocacy effort that the software applications used for advocacy outreach and engagement facilitates personalization of the message when contacting one's peers within their networks or their elected representatives.

Convenience of Mobilization

A critical objective of the process of engagement has always focused on the need for convenience. Make it easy, simple and convenient for anyone engaging with your advocacy project. This applies equally to donors, volunteers, other contributors, and media representatives. What do you ultimately want someone to do for your campaign, and how will they perform that task? For example, some campaigns incorporate online functionality in their websites that allows supporters to send messages directly to the elected representative in their jurisdiction.

Podcasts and Social Audio

Some people have compared podcasts to radio programs. While there are many similarities between the two, radio programs are broadcasts, sending a message in a "broad", non-specific way. The person behind the microphone is typically distanced from an audience. Podcasts are distributed digitally and specifically to listeners, one at a time. They are not broadcasts in any sense of the term. A radio program speaks to a larger, general audience with little or no listener interaction. Podcasts speak to listeners, typically in more intimate ways (such as personal earbuds), and are often defined by user engagement. Podcasts, by definition, are part of the world of social audio.

As we more thoroughly explored in Book II, some companies use podcasts to augment (and even replace) the corporate blog. Some local elected officials have regular podcast episodes that feature interviews with volunteers, owners of local businesses, student athletes, seniors, and others who comprise the community the official represents. As a delegate of the people, listeners hear that official responding to various opinions, providing a virtual town-hall. These podcasts are easily shared, uploaded to websites, and downloaded to a user's personal device. For those elected officials, the podcast helps reinforce the brand and profile in the community.

Podcasts tell stories from the human perspective; so they are, in many ways, ideal for issue advocacy. They are a source of information, as well as content that can feed directly into an organization's existing inventory of promotional and outreach tools.

Podcasts are also used to generate volunteers, using the passion of existing volunteers. Whether the organization is a political campaign, or church group that coordinates community events and food drives, volunteers are needed (and sometimes numbering in the hundreds). A podcast can help attract and recruit volunteers, that essential, make-or-break source of human passion and labour. Episodes can be hosted by volunteers. Alternatively, episodes can feature or highlight the experiences and stories of one or two volunteers in every episode. Podcasts can be used quite effectively as recruitment and retention vehicles.

One can also harness the social value of a podcast by creating discussion groups as an extension of the audio content. Forums like Reddit, Discord and Twitter are three examples of useful places to start. Clubhouse offers dedicated, often member-access only, social audio "rooms" with fully interactive conversation that can include anyone from anywhere. For those who use podcasting, such forums are wonderful sources of ideas, as well as for members/listeners to feel part of something more intimately connected to your campaign or project.

Listener engagement in a podcast and supporter mobilization in an advocacy campaign tend to be mutually reinforcing. Podcasts not only represent content; they are also a medium.

As with any content, user engagement can help define both the success of that content, as well as the form that any future or ongoing promotional efforts might take.

Complementarity with the "Old School"

To reiterate from Books I and II, research from Salesforce shows that consumers (individuals) prefer to receive promotional content through their email to a far greater degree than through any other form of communication. Email is a direct form of communication that can enable or empower the recipient. It can also last longer than a text message. User engagement through email should never be overlooked or considered "old school".

Opportunities and Challenges

Online and digital innovations in advocacy have proven to save money and time. Organizing twelve team members through a Zoom call, especially if those members reside in different cities or regions, is infinitely easier and cheaper than trying to coordinate a similar meeting in a physical setting - particularly if one or more of those team members has difficulty travelling. It is also considerably easier and more-cost effective than coordinating a teleconference. That said, there are a number of challenges associated with the increasing use of online and digital tools and methods.

The obvious challenge for many people is the lack of in-person interaction. We are accustomed to reading and responding to physical cues and body language, which does not transmit nearly as effectively through a digital application. Any sort of demonstration is also more challenging without an in-person interaction and exchange of feedback based on tactile experience. As much as possible, the use of online and digital interaction should be complemented with at least one gathering that is physical and in-person.

Another challenge with online and digital advocacy that some people might experience is found in the organizational dynamic and accompanying reporting structures. Advocacy teams that rely disproportionately on virtual methods tend to more closely resemble matrix-like organizations with matrix reporting structures (with multiple points of reporting and accountability). Not everyone is comfortable with matrix structures; and while not all virtual campaigns need to be featured by a matrix structure, the virtual nature of online campaigns tends to acquire matrix-like features.

These tools, methods and benefits very well may apply more naturally in the trade of lobbying advocacy, that realm often defined by larger financial stakes, more financially robust partners, and sometimes higher-level or more recent direct political expertise and experience. While individual support or membership can be instrumental in this realm, most players tend to be the larger and better-funded organizational types; unlike the world of primarily individual players, not all of whom may have access to digital and online tools, most organizational players probably would have such access. So, the benefits of these innovations may be more fully realized in a world characterized by a stronger presence of organizational players as opposed to smaller, individual types.

The Impact: Today and Tomorrow

Today, a successful advocacy professional generally must be able to effectively use the ever-widening array of digital tools and data to play both games strategically.

Increasingly, advocacy focuses on collecting data about consumer behavior and public opinion. Data collection can reveal many things, such as potential partners or allies not previously identified, or organizations that could be engaged in the issue and were previously not included.

At one time, building grassroots support meant engaging in public outreach to deepen support for the issue as well as to broaden the base of volunteers, members or supporters who could be mobilized to communicate with peers, media and public officer holders. As public policy has become more technical in many areas, and has therefore moved into more specialized, non-public forums of discussion, use of digital tools through social media, online networks and digital innovations (such as social audio or video) replace (to an extent) and augment the arenas where interest groups can attract publicity on an issue, and exert an amount of authority and influence. Social media and related online innovations have become important tools in advocacy campaigns, particularly those in which "buy-in" is deemed critical.

Additionally, the use of online networks facilitates a more comprehensive picture of the stakeholders and players in a given issue or cause. Advocacy and government relations professionals can now employ data-mining to obtain information that reveals the strengths and weaknesses of stakeholders and participants, either for or opposed to the issue or cause being promoted. Much like football coaches who scour over film footage of a player's strengths and weaknesses, professionals in advocacy also attempt to glean such information. Not only can information like this affect the quality and focus of the "conversation", it also creates a pivot for the next step.

Public relations, such as advertising, have typically been a consideration in many types of advocacy campaigns. Online methods of promotion and advertising can be less expensive, more targeted and potentially more effective.

Digital innovations have made an impact on public relations vis-a-vis the undeniable growth and importance of social media. If such tools are used effectively, by undergirding them with reliable data, the chances of success in the advocacy campaign increase multifold.

Digital and online innovations can help make an advocacy project more efficient and sometimes more cost-effective. The cautionary note reminds us that such innovations are tools; they are best used in a healthy mix of methods. Conceptualization of the problem and goal (or goals) at hand must always precede the choice of which tools to use. Knowing who your campaign is attempting to reach, and who the campaign is attempting to recruit as part of that effort, represent a key factor in determining which software and digital methods to use, including which tools (if any at all) are suitable to a given advocacy campaign. After all, one wouldn't likely employ a digital advocacy effort that relies on smartphones if the demographic group critical to the campaign were uncomfortable with, or couldn't afford to own, the technology.

9

Advocacy is formalized in the process of public policy making. Decision makers rely on feedback, input and expertise as part of the process of understanding how effective their programs, services and regulations will be. Advocacy, it could be said, is a communications input; public policy is the output.

More broad-based technology, which is also more widely available, has allowed anyone to become an advocacy mobilizer. The formalization of lobbying regulations, including the implementation of ever stricter rules, has added a legitimizing effect on the government relations and lobbying professions that at times have been the target for elimination. Almost every company today has in its employ or on retainer some sort of professional whose experience and expertise centres on government relations and lobbying. Rules and regulations have not reduced the number of people working in this field.

In fact, many governance structures themselves have incorporated the function of internal advocates. Advocates for seniors, children, women's issues, accessibility and disability issues, exist in the internal structure of many municipal and civic governments, for example. These positions serve almost like a watchdog, applying a lens filtered by the particular issue or cause. Such positions also help advance the issues, represented by their respective offices, throughout the government more generally. Even as high as the United Nations one finds internalized versions of advocacy: the Secretary-General, in addition to serving as a figure and symbol of the organization, is also "an advocate for all the world's peoples, especially the poor and vulnerable." (See UN website reference).

In most jurisdictions, lobbying (the codified form of advocacy and government relations) has been formalized into registration systems, providing a permit of sorts to apply one's craft of courting access and nurturing viewpoints more amenable to methods of persuasion. The growing link between communications input and the policy output is clearer and more defined than ever.

However, the balance of trust, accountability and the role of advocacy vis-a-vis the role of the elected body of representatives has not been maintained satisfactorily in the eyes of many critics. In fact, many would argue that the world of public policy decision making is characterized by an imbalance, with far too much "undue" and non-transparent influence by what many still consider to be "hucksters" or "palm greasers". For those who espouse this view, the term "lobbying" is a bad word.

Whenever one professional abuses the rules, exemptions and loopholes, it seems, new rules and restrictions are added. External lobbyists, internal government relations staff and advisory committees are all subject to greater scrutiny each time the regulations are reviewed by legislators. Paradoxically, for every new rule and regulation added (or tightened), the more codified the world of lobbying becomes; the more codified it becomes, the more it resembles a professional code. The increase of rules, definitions and regulatory compliance suggests not so much a way to "rein-in" the profession as much as it increasingly resembles a code of conduct, a requirement for professional membership, as it were. If only due to the increasing number of ever-stricter rules of compliance, lobbying specifically and advocacy more generally are not going to disappear. Regulators at all levels seem to have acknowledged and more formally recognized a legitimate role for advocacy in the communication-policy relationship.

Yet, there are changes afoot.

Changing Landscape of Community and Policy: Relatively Stronger, More Centralized Governments

The stage is set for bigger government. *The Economist* refers to this trend as a "great embiggening" (see "The great embiggening", November 20, 2021 issue).

The increasing demand for coordinated health care - as a direct result of rapidly aging populations - will lead to increases in government health spending; a prelude to this scenario looks to the spending and public infrastructure required for testing, control of mobility, and vaccination around the world during the covid-19 pandemic, infrastructures that will likely continue into the foreseeable future.

The growth is fueled by other policy areas as well: OECD agreements on a standardized level of corporate taxation and broad-based environmental and climate targets. On the climate front alone, the pledge by governments to eliminate net carbon transmissions necessarily adds to the expansion of state activity. Even deploying market mechanisms to achieve such policy goals will require an untold increase in regulatory measures. To put it bluntly, such policy targets require relatively stronger, more coordinated intervention by governments.

For these, and a host of other reasons, the trend worldwide shows a tendency for stronger, more centralized governments. The larger and more ambitious the policy goals, the larger and more robust the governments will be that are tasked with managing and overseeing the systems that work towards achieving those goals. One of the key changes to the landscape of community and policy will not focus on the nature of state activity, but on the size and reach; as governments, which will continue to face unrelenting pressures to employ an ever greater mix of policy tools through increasingly coordinated (and possibly centralized) means.

More 'Public' in Public Policy

The "back rooms" of politics were once a defining feature in the field of influencers. Today, this feature is less common among those defined as lobbyists. Lobbying legislation has helped increase levels of transparency (or, at least, a degree of translucency). Moreover, public affairs are, quite literally, more public than ever. Online networks, virtual communities and social media can make as profound a change (and sometimes more so) to the governing agenda than traditional methods of advancing an issue or cause. Traditional methods relied almost exclusively on an individual's networking skills and expertise of certain policy sectors, decision makers and participants. Increasingly, those hoping to lead a charge in making political or policy change will need to embrace the newer tools of public affairs, namely online networks, the use of virtual communities, and social media.

One's chances of making desired change to a regulation, law or policy are seriously diminished without a fluent, working knowledge of digital organizing, mobilizing and content promotion. This trend will also continue to see more grassroots groups forming, and using the tools that are easily accessed, to build an activist momentum to effect political or policy change.

New Players in Alliances, Partnerships and Coalitions

At one time, groups or companies joined together to speak with a singular voice through an industry association when engaged in advancing issues or causes in the political arena. These were usually industry-based or sector-based. Increasingly, intersectionality is the buzzword and go-to model of organization, a model that now recognizes much broader communities are at play when organizing to advance a cause. New players include civic groups and representatives, groups that can potentially exert considerable authority (the rise and impact of online networks and communities popularly termed "cancel culture", for example).

Counter-lobbying

Lee Drutman, a prolific author on the topic of lobbying, argues that more lobbying is a better solution to the imbalance in governance, characterized by the shadowy world of political influence, than attempts to eliminate or restrict lobbying. He suggests a notion called "public lobbyists", positions that would be appointed by the US Congress (his discussion falls within the US context, but a comparable approach could be envisaged for other counties). The largely underfunded causes, many of them social, charitable or non-profit in nature, could receive the assistance of a publicly-funded lobbyist to advance their positions and issues. Publicly-funded lobbyists would operate in ways not dissimilar to the position of the public defender, and help ensure that everyone gets a voice at the political and policy table. Referring to the concept as counter-lobbying, Drutman argues that such positions could represent affirmative steps towards achieving greater balance among the influencers.

Another approach to counter-lobbying is seen through the growth of citizen-based movements, largely online and virtual, that use social media and digital mobilizing tools. Such tools and software have made the task of influencing more affordable, more accessible to more groups, and ultimately more contributory to participatory democracy. When coordinated effectively, such lobbying movements not only serve to counter the traditional "big business" lobby, but they also potentially reach many more people, and broaden their points of policy and political influence, through rapid-fire techniques characteristic of online viral messaging.

A Redefined Role and Nature of the State: Corporations as the Target of Advocacy

Some passionate interests who have sought change have not focused on government, but have identified the corporate world as the source of authority. Advocacy organizers increasingly point to non-government entities to generate the changes they seek.

For example, recent efforts to "police" illicit pornography as well as the activities of far-right groups have ignored legislators entirely. These efforts have focused on companies like

Mastercard, a global credit-card company. Instead of engaging with public office holders in an attempt to introduce or refine internet regulation (if, indeed, this is even practicable), activists have taken their efforts to the forum of corporate shareholders and the company board. If a company like Mastercard blocked payments to far-right groups, for example, the feasibility is reduced for such groups to find real estate and build momentum on the Internet (See "Credit card firms are becoming reluctant regulators" *The Economist*).

Similar efforts have impacted branding decisions of universities, corporate entities and individual products as a result of similar lobbying efforts that did not even consider the role and efficacy of government entities.

The target of lobbying might also see advocacy and activist groups becoming members of the corporations they wish to influence by way of purchasing shares – thereby acquiring the right to vote and raise issues as a shareholder. This is a practice that could perhaps be termed, "very direct, yet indirect, non-public office holder advocacy".

Increasingly, the authority and power of the corporate world in some spheres (and the diminution or inaction of government in those same spheres) has the potential for advocacy to expand significantly beyond the traditional landscape of governance. Should the authority over public policy shift from government to the corporate entity, then so, too, will the practice of organized influencing (which, presumably, will add to perspectives around the terms lobbying and government relations advocacy).

The Landscape, Tools, Methods and Partners Change, but the Song of Advocacy Remains the Same

Whether lobbyists work for a large organization, a private individual, or the general public, their goals and strategies are the same: exerting influence to change the political or policy agenda.

As an integral component in the relationship between communication and policy, the lobbyist must be adept at the art of persuasion. Despite any changes in the landscape or the rules regulating the profession, advocacy professionals will still need to focus on how to sway politicians to vote on legislation in a way that favours the interests they represent.

Achieve Greater Balance

Recalling the tales and legends from earlier chapters, the term "lobbyist" derives from the location where early lobbyists worked - the lobbies or anterooms of political and legislative buildings. As the fourth President of the United States, James Madison, warned in his writings, bribery is a constant threat lurking in the activity of lobbying. In fact, bribery was rampant in earlier times. The lobbyist at that time was a less transparent, shadier and darker figure, whose role in communication and policy was, nonetheless, consequential in many regards.

Since the time of Madison (and others, as the term "lobbying" is attributed to many similar origins and individuals), tighter rules and more clearly defined legislation have helped achieve agreed-upon systems that result in at least a little more balance between the influence of advocacy professionals and elected legislators. Recent laws, for example, require companies to disclose their lobbyists' names and report all gifts given to public office holders (many rules even restrict the value of such gifts). Mandated delays are also more common. The mandated delay - the time between when a person ceasing to hold public office and when that same individual returns to the centres of legislative decision making as an advocacy professional - is a measure intended to address the process known as the "revolving door".

Achieving greater balance is always desirable. That said, advocacy efforts in general, and specific forms that include lobbying, cannot be legislated out of existence. As long as legislation and decision makers exist, there will be constituents, stakeholders and interested parties, and assorted professionals in the field of government relations and advocacy, who have a legitimate role to play in informing public policy.

Efforts to achieve greater balance might consider the application of universal definitions that capture all interaction between public office holders and non-government parties, thereby broadening the definition (and minimizing the confusion) about what a lobbyist is and does.

To do so would require a transition from the current practice prescribed by government definitions that quantify types of activity to one that qualifies who is an influencer. Granted, this approach is not without conceptual and practical challenges. But such an approach could move beyond the narrow (and somewhat arbitrary) definitions, originally introduced as reactions, and aimed at ferreting out unscrupulous activity, to a system that more holistically captures the reality of today's processes that inform and shape public policy and legislation. The role of influencers, be they lobbyists, government relations specialists or activists, is likely to increase.

10

James Abrams Garfield is likely not a name that most people would know much about. He was the 20th US president, the second to be assassinated, and the third to die while in office. He was also one of several, including John Quincy Adams, James Madison, and William McKinley (who, incidentally was the third to be assassinated), who wanted to tackle the practice of lobbying in a meaningful and sustainable way. Garfield's case is perhaps closer to the world of those interested in lobbying and government affairs: the bullet that ultimately took his life was fired by a disgruntled man who believed the President owed him a political appointment to a government position. Especially in the 1880s, lobbying and patronage often accompanied the political cycles. In Garfield's case, it was the appointment process and the public administration that were foremost. Garfield hoped to sever the machinery of government from any form of political influence. Following his death, Chester A. Arthur, Garfield's Vice-President, and another name that most people likely know little about, assumed the presidency. Among his first initiatives was the passage of the Pendleton Civil Service Reform Act, legislation that mandated meritocracy in the civic service and the consequent removal of most positions within the federal government (at that time) from the influence of political lobbying and political patronage.

Lobbying rules, as we see today, even outright anti-lobbying legislation, likely would not have made a difference in the tragic outcome for Garfield (the "disgruntled" wielder of the gun was later deemed "unstable"). Yet this fact did not lessen the perceived need to remove certain realms of employment positions from the reach of patronage and possible lobbying. The Act was swiftly passed under the presidential signature of Arthur; as even the perception of being awarded an appointment in return for political support was an outstanding issue of the day, hastened by the killing of Garfield.

The impact of lobbying has been featured in countless films, including early classics like *Mr. Smith Goes to Washington* (1939) and *All the King's Men* (1949). Such depictions showed political systems and political leaders all too often working at the behest of professional lobbyists and their clients. Recent news stories in the UK seem to feature the negative side of lobbying more in fact than in fiction: "The facts are damning," reports *The Economist* (See "Political Lobbying", *The Economist*, November 6, 2021). "Owen Paterson, a former Tory Cabinet minister now on the backbenches, was paid….$12,700[US] a month for consulting work by two companies, one and a half times his parliamentary salary. And sure enough, he earned his keep by lobbying ministers and officials on their behalf. The commissioner for standards, an independent officer, concluded that he had brought Parliament into disrepute." Even in the industry itself, despite the prevalence of the lobbying specialization in the world of advocacy, it is interesting how few professionals actually refer to themselves as lobbyists (often preferring presumably friendlier terms like government relations specialists or public affairs advisors).

It is not surprising that the connotation (and, in some jurisdictions, the legal definition of the practice) of lobbying is often equated with nefariousness, skullduggery, and political backroom deals that serve to benefit primarily the immediate individuals involved. It is also interesting to note that the connotation of advocacy evokes a more generous, benevolent and charitable image, with the benefits of such a practice extended to larger (sometimes marginalized) groups in society. Yet, both practices often overlap in their methods, techniques and tactics, although, in reality, not usually as profoundly as depicted in classic Hollywood motion pictures.

Despite the popular and enduring image, and the stigma associated with it, lobbying is a form of advocacy. It is undeniably the most publicly well-known of all forms of attempting to influence the policy and political agendas. It is also that type of practice that has been subject to the ire of political critics and many elected officials since at least the days when the role of government management and public administration expanded considerably beyond its initial focus of areas such as protecting the ports and directing military efforts. Direct, corporate lobbying began to really take shape as soon as governments began making decisions that entailed some consequence for a company's goods, services or operations. Advocacy, as a term, precedes the coining of the term lobbyist; yet it was the lobbyist who became that inadvertent policy actor who accompanied the increasing role, size and nature scope of the state.

Advocacy dates back much further (with Lady Godiva used as one example). Earlier discussion highlighted many of the sources of confusion and trajectories of similarity between advocacy and lobbying. Yet, advocacy as a practice has never raised the ire of elected representatives (at least to the same degree) as lobbying.

Clarify the Concepts, Practices and Terminology

Most political critics and observers tend to agree that lobbying legislation provides anyone interested an opportunity to scrutinize activity reports submitted to the government. The laws provide a degree of illumination (not quite transparency) into some of the paper trails between the public office holder and the individual who seeks to influence the governing or political system in some way. The rules also tend to provide somewhat of a "membership roster", a who's who, in the realm of direct communication with public office holders.

Yet such legislation has further legitimized the practice that many have sought to eliminate -

if, for no other reason, that the terminology and definitions do not capture the breadth and depth of the practice. The reason: because lobbying is simply part of a much broader practice of advocacy.

Why not clarify our concepts, practices and terminology? The focus should be on advocacy; only then can we appropriately consider which specific forms of advocacy are acceptable and which are not.

Advocacy can take many shapes, and is described with many terms. There is grassroots lobbying and grassroots advocacy. Then there is direct lobbying and indirect lobbying. Some lobbyists have chosen to use the term government relations specialist or public relations specialist. We've seen many examples of political activism in recent decades, the object of which is raise awareness or change public perception, often entailing the recruitment or endorsement of a public official; yet such practices are rarely termed lobbying. Despite differences in approach, method, technique or tactic, all of these are types of advocacy.

First Principles

Who exactly are we trying to capture when addressing the world of "lobbyists"? What exactly are we trying to do by having these lobbyists register and report to government? What is the goal of such public policy?

There is no single answer. Which is one reason why the definitions (and their applications) of the rules and regulations, aside from providing a publicly-accessible paper trail, have limited relevance and effectiveness.

Most would probably agree that the specific practice that is usually the target of anti-lobbying initiatives is bribery. Still others aim to include patronage as a target for anti-lobbying laws, which is the case in some jurisdictions, and increasingly a practice considered inconsistent with current acceptable standards and ethics.

Yet it really comes down to transparency. Most codes and regulations that govern lobbying practices (even those in some countries that extend to advocacy in general) are designed to publicly reveal the players, meetings and content shared.

A World of Difference

These are some countries, such as Canada and the United States, which employ transparency and accountability measures in ways that are not entirely dissimilar. However, a survey across many countries around the globe reveals more differences. Achieving greater clarity on whom and what is captured under legislation really seems to take many forms, using many differing definitions, and is a collection of processes that are characterized by inconsistency more than anything else.

Consider *Lobbyists, Governments and Public Trusts*, a study by the Organization for Economic Cooperation and Development (OECD), which reveals a number of deficiencies and exemptions in national attempts to achieve greater transparency and accountability:

> *Lobbying activities are usually defined as oral, written and electronic communications between public officials and lobbyists. The specific types of*

> *communications covered are not always clearly defined, and what constitutes "direct" and "indirect" influence is also not explicitly defined. In certain countries, technical guidance documents further clarify the scope of lobbying. For example, the website of the Irish lobbying register indicates that "relevant communications" can include informal communications such as casual encounters, social gatherings, social media messages directed to public officials, or "grassroots" communication, defined as an activity where an organisation instructs its members or supporters to contact public officials on a particular matter. Similarly, the UK Office of the Registrar of Consultant Lobbyists indicates that social media messages directed to an official or personal account fits the criteria for consultant lobbying and requires registration. Many activities, however, are still exempt from transparency requirements. (See OECD, Lobbyists, Governments and Public Trusts)*

Invitations by public officials are often exempt. As the OECD study points out, this is the case in Australia, the US and Peru, for example. In contrast, France excludes grassroots advocacy campaigns, as well as and public efforts that are defined as public awareness projects, from its regulatory reach. Anything considered advisory is also exempt from regulation in the US, Germany and Chile (except sometimes when a charitable tax status is associated with the group conducting the advocacy). In Chile and the United States, for example, invitations from public office holders to individuals to participate in meetings of a "technical" nature exempt the professionals in question.

Ireland's attempts to advance transparency have moved in the opposite direction, including policy working groups. Citing the OECD report again, "interactions between members of policy working groups are exempt from lobbying transparency requirements only if the working group adheres to the Transparency Code (published on the website of the Standards in Public Office Commission), which requires the group to publish the membership, terms of reference, agendas and minutes of meetings."

Then there are those passionate groups who have attempted to eliminate or ban lobbying altogether, whose efforts have not achieved the intended results. The best they have been able to achieve is imposing compliance procedures that increase transparency and heighten accountability (which is a commendable goal in itself).

Recognizing that lobbying is a form of advocacy, the question becomes: should the broader practice of advocacy be eliminated (and not just lobbying), or should advocacy be embraced as a fully functioning, contributory part of the public policy system, and, accordingly, fall within the capture of legislation that is currently characterized by more exemptions than it is by applications?

Transparency

More transparency is needed in all forms of influence. The lines between those groups and practices that are exempt from lobbying legislation are increasingly blurred against those groups and practices that are captured by the legislation. Should payment be a defining criterion? In other words, should volunteers be captured in legislation (as they currently are not in a number of jurisdictions)? What about church and religious organizations, schools, non-profits and other NGOs? Furthermore, some jurisdictions exempt government representatives while others capture those individuals as well. For example, should a State governor or Provincial premier be subject to rules of transparency in those instances when the individual tours the political and business representatives in other jurisdictions in an attempt to generate interest and investment in their home State or Province? Some accountability rules differentiate between meetings that are on the public record compared to those that are considered private. When the meeting is considered private, even a non-profit representative in Canada is required to register and submit activity reports. Should the details of such private meetings of elected officials receive the same public scrutiny?

To provide transparency and allow for public scrutiny, anyone considered a proponent of lobbying legislation should be asked to clearly define the term "lobbying" with a robust, comprehensive and sufficiently explicit definition to avoid misinterpretation and to prevent loopholes. Furthermore, clarity is required as regards core disclosure requirements, which should identify the beneficiaries of lobbying, and that supplementary disclosure requirements should shed light on where lobbying pressures and funding come from. In sum, a more comprehensive approach to defining lobbying is necessary to cover the influence of the policymaking process in all its forms.

Greater Transparency in All Forms of Influence

There are several areas where transparency is not advanced by lobbying legislation. Transparency on core lobbying activities is limited. Transparency is generally limited on the sources of funds for research, think tanks and grassroots organisations (if they apply at all). More transparency is needed on the use of media, social media and related online and digital innovations as lobbying tools. Transparency is limited as regards one-off communication from interests advising government. Moreover, transparency on core lobbying activities is limited in many jurisdictions.

Whether our efforts focus on improving the system that regulates professionals whose vocation is the art of influence, or reforming it altogether, our first principles should focus on advocacy in general, and enhancing the practices and procedures that illuminate how public policy and legislation is introduced, changed or eliminated.

Recognize the role and contributions of advocacy, and formally include all players and participants in the process of public policy making. Bottom line: if you participate somehow in the systems that influence public policy and legislation, then you are a contributor who should be identified in publicly accountable ways.

The Art of Influence: Advocacy's Role in Participatory Democracy

Advocacy (be it grassroots, direct lobbying or online mobilization) increasingly represents a key input into productive and effective government. Without that input, government decision makers would be undeniably weaker in their attempts to design policy options that are responsive, meaningful and sustainable. Advocacy efforts help provide access to legislators, and can serve as valuable educational tools.

Advocacy efforts also help maintain momentum and awareness of issues and causes. They help raise the volume, so to speak, and help keep the volume high enough to retain the attention of public office holders. Government decision makers are faced with countless issues when considering policy options, and advocacy efforts help maintain certain issues as priority issues.

Advocacy efforts help address potential deficiencies and gaps in knowledge. When presenting their case, advocacy professionals provide experiential research, sector-specific data, and industry feedback and opinion. Such ingredients are critical to the success of any effective public policy measure. In other words, advocacy professionals help insert, and reinforce the importance of, the public in public policy.

A Fresh Perspective on Advocacy

The specific practice of lobbying has been the target of lawmakers for generations. Most legislators have tried to avoid implicating advocacy professionals in general; yet, despite healthy intentions, the results are often confusing and muddled. Legislative attempts to address the practice of lobbying have largely been reactionary (as exemplified by the extreme case of the assignation of a former US President discussed earlier). Reactive policy can be hailed as responding to public concern, pressing issues and causes. However, reactive policy is seldom featured by forward-looking perspectives that thoughtfully conceptualize what exactly the problem is; instead, the measures selected are typically chosen for the sake of political expediency, as opposed to the efficacy of policy.

A more fulsome approach to the art of influence is needed: one that balances the role of elected representatives; one that embraces and celebrates the contributory role that advocacy can (and often does) have in the formulation of public policy; one that facilitates the advancement of causes from virtually any sector or realm of society, without creating undo administrative or compliance burdens or new apparatuses of public administration; one that is harmonized as much as possible across and within jurisdictions - and, ideally, one that will create more clarity and better understanding of the terms "grassroots activism", "lobbying" and "advocacy".

A few final words. No advocacy campaign is complete without an appreciation of the principles and lessons of content creation and promotion. Advocacy, and it various forms, as we have seen, can be technical and detailed. For those seeking a fuller treatment of advocacy, consider reading *Advocacy-Explained!* in its entirety as a stand-alone book. For those wanting to maximize their advocacy efforts, remember that these extend from content creation; and remember to embrace the essential techniques of communication, promotion and outreach – in which podcasting and audio technologies are now centrally positioned.

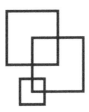

REFERENCES AND FURTHER READING

BOOK I: CONTENT CREATION AND PROMOTION

Barnum, P.T. *Barnum's Own Story: The Autobiography of P.T. Barnum*. New York: Dover Publications, 2017.

Champion, Justin. *Inbound Content: A Step-by-Step Guide to Doing Content Marketing the Inbound Way*. Hoboken: Wiley, 2018.

Diehl, Gregory V. *Brand Identity Breakthrough: How to Craft Your Company's Unique Story to Make Your Products Irresistible*. Buffalo, Wyoming: Identity Publications, 2016.

Handley, Ann. *Everybody Writes: Your Go-To Guide to Creating Ridiculously Good Content*. Hoboken: Wiley, 2014.

Hanly, Laura. *Content That Converts: How to Build a Profitable and Predictable B2B Content Marketing Strategy*. Self-published, CreateSpace Independent Publishing Platform, 2016.

Heifetz, Ronald A., Marty Linsky and Alexander Grashow. *Practice of Adaptive Leadership: Tools and Tactics for Changing Your Organization and the World*. Brighton, Massachusetts: Harvard Business Review Press, 2009.

"Internalizing Externalities." *The Economist*. Special

report on ESG investing. July 23, 2022. https://www.economist.com/special-report/2022/07/21/internalising-the-externalities

Johnson, Matt and Prince Ghuman. *Blindsight: The (Mostly) Hidden Ways Marketing Reshapes Our Brains.* Dallas: BenBella Books, 2020.

Lund, Kevin. *Conversation Marketing: How to be Relevant and Engage Your Customer by Speaking Human.* Newburyport, MA: Weiser, 2018.

Norris, Dan. *Content Machine: Use Content Marketing to Build a 7-Figure Business with Zero Advertising.* Self-published, CreateSpace Independent Publishing Platform, 2015.

Pulizzi, Joe. *Epic Content Marketing: How to Tell a Different Story, Break through the Clutter, and Win More Customers by Marketing Less.* New York: McGraw-Hill Education, 2013.

Schaefer, Mark W. *The Content Code: 6 Essential Strategies to Ignite Your Content, Your Marketing, and Your Business.* Self-published, 2015.

Sheridan, Marcus. *They Ask, You Answer: A Revolutionary Approach to Inbound Sales, Content Marketing, and Today's Digital Consumer.* Hoboken: Wiley, 2019.

Wilson, Pamela. *Master Content Strategy: How to Maximize Your Reach & Boost Your Bottom Line Every Time You Hit Publish.* Nashville: BIG Brand Books, 2018.

BOOK II: PODCASTING

Abel, Jessica. *Out on the Wire: The Storytelling Secrets of the New Masters of Radio.* New York: Crown, 2015.

Bartlett, Richard A. *The World of Ham Radio, 1901-1950: A Social History.* Jefferson, NC: McFarland Publishing, 2015.

Berger, J. *Contagious: Why Things Catch On.* New York: Simon & Schuster, 2013.

Calder, B. J., Malthouse, E. C., Schaedel, U. "An experimental study of the relationship between online engagement and advertising effectiveness". *Journal of Interactive Marketing.* 23. 2009.

Clark, Clay and Marshall Morris. *Podcast Creation 101: The Proven Path to Podcasting Success.* Swanage, UK: Madness Media, 2018.

Dumas, John Lee. *Podcast Launch.* Self-Published. CreateSpace Independent Publishing Platform, 2015.

Dunning, John. *On the Air: The Encyclodedia of Old-Time Radio*. Oxford, UK: Oxford University Press, 1998.

Garratt, GRM. *The Early History of Radio: From Faraday to Marconi (History and Management of Technology)*. Stevenage, UK: The Institution of Engineering and Technology, 1994.

Hethmon, Hannah. *Your Museum Needs a Podcast: A Step-By-Step Guide to Podcasting on a Budget for Museums, History Organizations, and Cultural Nonprofits*. Self-published, 2018.

Hunt, Daniel. *Podcasting for Beginners: How to Start and Grow a Successful and Profitable Podcast*. London: Flaneur Media, 2020.

Jackson, Dave. *Profit from Your Podcast: Proven Strategies to Turn Listeners into a Livelihood*. New York: Allworth, 2020.

Kern, Jonathan. *Sound Reporting: The NPR Guide to Audio Journalism and Production*. Chicago: University of Chicago Press, 2008.

Lehmann, J., Lalmas, M., Yom-Tov, E., Dupret, G. "Models of user engagement". In Masthoff, J., Mobasher, B., Desmarais, M. C., Nkambou, R. (Eds.), *User Modeling, Adaptation, and Personalization* (pp. 164-175). Berlin: Springer. 2012.

Mayo, Amanda. *Podcasting: How to Start a Podcast and Create a Profitable Podcasting Business*. Self-published, 2019.

Mazzoni, Dominic. *Podcasting with Audacity: Creating a Podcast with Free Audio Software*. London: Pearson Education, 2007.

McLuhan, Marshall. *The Medium Is the Massage: An Inventory of Effects*. London: Penguin Books, 1967.

McLuhan, Marshall. *Understanding Media*. New York: McGraw Hill Education, 1964.

Meinzer, Kristen. *So You Want to Start a Podcast: Finding Your Voice, Telling Your Story, and Building a Community That Will Listen*. New York: William Morrow, 2019.

Napoli, P. M. *Audience Evolution: New Technologies and the Transformation of Media Audiences*. New York: Columbia University Press, 2011.

Nuzum, Eric. *Make Noise: A Creator's Guide to Podcasting and Great Audio Storytelling*. New York: Workman Publishing Company, 2019.

O'Brien, H. L., Toms, E. G. "What is user engagement? A conceptual framework for defining user engagement with technology". *Journal of the American Society for Information Science and Technology*, 59. 2008.

Penn, Joanna. *Audio For Authors: Audiobooks, Podcasting, and Voice Technologies*. Bath, UK: Curl Up Press, 2020.

Rossing, Thomas D. and Neville H. Fletcher. *Principles of Vibration and Sound*. New York: Springer Publishing, 2004.

Sullivan, John L. "The Platforms of Podcasting: Past and Present". *Social Media + Society*. Vol. 5, No. 4. November 28, 2019.

Van Cour, Shawn. *Making Radio: Early Radio Production and the Rise of Modern Sound Culture*. Audio Book Narrated by Timothy Andrés Pabon. Oxford, UK: Oxford University Press, 2018.

BOOK III: ADVOCACY

Alemanno, Alberto. *Lobbying for Change: Find Your Voice to Create a Better Society*. Cambridge, UK. Icon Books Ltd, 2017.

Alinsky, Saul. *Rules for Radicals: A Pragmatic Primer for Realistic Radicals*. New York: Vintage, 1989.

Anastasiadis, Stephanos. "Understanding Corporate Lobbying on its Own Terms." *ICCSR Research Paper Series, No. 42-2006*. International Centre for Corporate Social Responsibility, Nottingham

University Business School, 2006.

Avner, Marcia. *The Lobbying and Advocacy Handbook for Nonprofit Organizations, Second Edition: Shaping Public Policy at the State and Local Level.* St. Paul, MN: Fieldstone Alliance Publishing, 2013.

Baumgartner, Frank R., Jeffrey M. Berry, Marie Hojnacki, et. al. *Lobbying and Policy Change: Who Wins, Who Loses, and Why.* Chicago: University of Chicago Press, 2009.

BBC News. "Boris Johnson follows Labour call to ban MP paid adviser jobs." *BBC Online.* November 16, 2021. https://www.bbc.com/news/uk-politics-59311003.

BBC News. "Lobbying: Call for greater transparency around access to ministers." *BBC Online.* June 13, 2021. https://www.bbc.com/news/uk-politics-57457852.

BBC News. "What is lobbying? A brief guide." *BBC Online.* November 5, 2021. https://www.bbc.com/news/uk-politics-56733456.

Bennett, Cory. "Johnson's handling of UK lobbying row is 'shameful,' says ex-UK PM". *Politico.* November 6, 2021. https://www.politico.eu/article/boris-johnson-uk-lobbying-row-shameful-john-major/.

Bhatnagar, Khyati. "Why Does India Not Regulate Lobbying Under Its Legislation?" *Youth Ki Awaaz*. October 31, 2018.

Birnbaum, Jeffrey. *The Lobbyists: How Influence Peddlers Work Their Way in Washington*. Toronto: Penguin Random House, 2015.

Blau, B., T. Brough and D. Thomas (2013), "Corporate lobbying, political connections, and the bailout of banks," *Journal of Banking & Finance*, Vol. 37/8, pp. `3007-3017, https://doi.org/10.1016/j.jbankfin.2013.04.005.

Boris, Elizabeth T. and C. Eugene Steuerle, Eds. *Nonprofits and Government: Collaboration and Conflict*. Washington, DC: Rowman and Littlefield Publishers, 2016.

Canada. *Lobbying Act of Canada (R.S.C., 1985, c. 44 (4th Supp.))* https://laws-lois.justice.gc.ca/eng/acts/l-12.4/.

Cao, Zhiyan, Guy D. Fernando, Arindam Tripathy and Arun Upadhyay. "The Economics of Corporate Lobbying." *Journal of Corporate Finance*. Volume 49, 2018, pp 54-80.

Carter, Terrance S. and Ryan M. Prendergrast. "What Charities and NFPs Need to Know for the

Upcoming Federal Election." *Charity and NFP Law Bulletin No. 499*. Carters, August 25, 2021. https://www.carters.ca/pub/bulletin/charity/2021/chylb499.pdf.

Christianson, Steven. *Content Creation and Promotion – Explained!.* Toronto: Henley Point, 2021.

Clahane, Patrick, Brian Wheeler & Matt Murphy. "All-party groups: The source of the next Westminster lobbying scandal?" *BBC News*. https://www.bbc.com/news/uk-politics-59307270.

Cnockaert, Jesse. "Lobbyists can get 'too caught up in the specifics' volunteering with election campaigns, says Fasken partner." *The Hill Times*. August 16, 2021. www.hilltimes.com/2021/08/16/lobbyists-can-get-too-caught-up-in-the-specifics-volunteering-with-election-campaigns-says-fasken-partner/311898.

Drutman, Lee. "How Corporate Lobbyists Conquered American Democracy: Business didn't always have so much power in Washington." *The Atlantic*. April 20, 2015. Online Edition. www.theatlantic.com/business/archive/2015/04/how-corporate-lobbyists-conquered-american-democracy/390822/.

Drutman, Lee. *The Business of America is Lobbying: How Corporation Became Politicized and Politics Became More Corporate.* London, UK: Oxford University Press, 2015.

Drutman, Lee. "The solution to lobbying is more lobbying." *The Washington Post.* April 29, 2015. https://www.washingtonpost.com/news/monkey-cage/wp/2015/04/29/the-solution-to-lobbying-is-more-lobbying/.

European Parliament. "Lobby Groups and Transparency." https://www.europarl.europa.eu/at-your-service/en/transparency/lobby-groups.

European Parliament Think Tank. "New lobbying law in France." July 4, 2018. https://europarl.europa.eu/thinktank/en/document.html?reference=EPRS_BRI(2018)625104.

Fitch, Brad. *Citizen's Handbook to Influencing Elected Officials: Citizen Advocacy in State Legislatures and Congress.* Alexandria, Virginia: TheCapitol.Net, 2010.

Gelak, Deanna. *Lobbying and Advocacy: Winning Strategies, Resources, Recommendations, Ethics and Ongoing Compliance for Lobbyists and Washington Advocates: The Best of Everything Lobbying and Washington Advocacy.* Alexandria, Virginia:

TheCapitol.Net, 2008.

Geiger M.E.S, Dr. Andreas. *EU Lobbying Handbook*. Independently published, 2012.

Giono, Guy. "New Lobbyists' Code Will Restrict Dealings with Canada's Federal Government and Agencies." Canadian Bar Association. https://www.cba.org/Blast-Emails/Communications/PracticeLink/Seen-and-Noted/New-Lobbyists-Code-will-restrict-dealings-with-Ca.

Honest Leadership and Open Government Act of 2007 (Pub. L. 110-81, 121 Stat. 735 - September 14).

Influence Map (2020), "Corporate lobbying: how companies really impact progress on climate." https://influencemap.org/climate-lobbying.

Jacob, Dr. Kathryn Allamong. *King of the Lobby: The Life and Times of Sam Ward, Man-About-Washington in the Gilded Age.* Baltimore: Johns Hopkins University Press, 2009.

Johnson, Dennis W. *No Place for Amateurs: How Political Consultants are Reshaping American Democracy.* Abingdon, UK: Routledge, 2001.

Kaiser, Robert. *So Damn Much Money: The Triumph of Lobbying and the Corrosion of American Government.* New York: Vintage Publishing, 2010.

Kavuchak, Andrew. *The Fight for Autism Treatment in Canada: Reflections of a Parent Activist.* Independently published. 2020.

Korte, Gregory, Naomi Nix and Ben Brody. "Biden Imposes New Restrictions on Corporate Lobbying." *Bloomberg.com.* January 20, 2021. www.bloomberg.com/news/articles/2021-01-20/biden-to-impose-new-restrictions-on-corporate-lobbying.

LaPira, Timothy and Herschel F. Thomas. *Revolving Door Lobbying Public Service, Private Influence, and the Unequal Representation of Interests.* Lawrence, Kansas: University Press of Kansas, 2017.

Libby, Patricia. *The Lobbying Strategy Handbook: 10 Steps to Advancing Any Cause Effectively.* Thousand Oaks, California: Sage Publications, 2011.

Lobbying Disclosure Act of 1995. 109 STAT. 691. Public Law 104-65, 104th Congress of the United States. www.govinfo.gov/content/pkg/STATUTE-109/pdf/STATUTE-109-Pg691.pdf.

Machiavelli, Nicollo, Anthony Grafton and George Bull. *The Prince.* Toronto: Penguin (Reissue), 2003.

Miller, David and William Dinan. "Corridors of Power: Lobbying in the UK," *Observatoire de la société britannique* [Online], 6 | 2008, Online since

01 February 2001.

http://journals.openedition.org/osb/409
https://doi.org/10.4000/osb.409.

Miller-Stevens, Katrina and Matthew J. Gable. "Lobbying in the Virtual World: Perceptions in the Nonprofit Sector." *Nonprofit Policy Forum*, vol. 4, no. 1, 2013, pp. 47-63.
https://doi.org/10.1515/npf-2012-0002.

Minjeong, K., C. Joo Chung and J. Hyun Kim (2011), "Who shapes network neutrality policy debate? An examination of information subsidizers in the mainstream media and at Congressional and FCC hearings," *Telecommunications Policy*, Vol. 35/4, pp. 314-324,
https://doi.org/10.1016/j.telpol.2011.02.005.

Moore, Mark H. *Creating Public Value: Strategic Management in Government.* Cambridge, MA: Harvard University Press, 1995.

Mullins, Brody. "President Trump Rescinds Own Lobbying Ban." *The Wall Street Journal.* January 20, 2021.
https://www.wsj.com/articles/president-trump-rescinds-own-lobby-ban-11611156215.

National Conference of State Legislatures (NCSL). "How States Define Lobbying and Lobbyist." https://www.ncsl.org/research/ethics/50-statechart-lobby-definitions.aspx.

Obama, Barrack. 2009. *Executive Order No. 13490*, January 21.

OECD. "Lobbying in the 21st Century: Transparency, Integrity and Access." https://www.oecd-ilibrary.org/sites/8b6ec100-en/index.html?itemId=/content/component/8b6ec100-en.

OECD (2014), *Lobbyists, Governments and Public Trust, Volume 3: Implementing the OECD Principles for Transparency and Integrity in Lobbying*, OECD Publishing, Paris, https://dx.doi.org/10.1787/9789264214224-en.

Office of the Conflict of Interest and Ethics Commissioner. "International Panel Hosted by Members of European Parliament Highlighted Ethics and Lobbying Frameworks in France and Canada." Ottawa: March 31, 2021. https://ciec-ccie.parl.gc.ca/en/news-nouvelles/Pages/NREU.aspx.

Pal, Leslie. *Beyond Policy Analysis – Public Issue Management in Turbulent Times*, Fifth Edition. Toronto: Nelson Education, 2014.

"Plastic policemen: Credit card firms are becoming reluctant regulators of the web." Finance and Economics. *The Economist*. October 16th-22nd,

2021. https://www.economist.com/finance-and-economics/credit-card-firms-are-becoming-reluctant-regulators-of-the-web/21805450.

"Political Lobbying: Tory Sleaze Again." *The Economist*. November 6, 2021. https://www.economist.com/britain/2021/11/06/britains-government-goes-to-disgraceful-lengths-to-protect-a-tory-mp.

Pross, A. Paul. "Lobbying in Canada." *The Canadian Encyclopedia*. February 7, 2006. https://www.thecanadianencyclopedia.ca/en/article/lobbying.

Purves, Grant and Jack Stilborn. *Members of the House of Commons: Their Role, BP-56E*. Ottawa: December 1988 (Revised June 1997). https://publications.gc.ca/.

Sabatier, P. A. "Policy Change Over a Decade or More." In P. A. Sabatier and H. Jenkins-Smith (Eds.) *Policy Change and Learning: An Advocacy Coalition Approach* (pp. 13-39). Boulder, CO: Westview, 1993.

Savoie, Donald. "Canada's political institutions are failing: The next parliament must save them." *Globe and Mail*. September 20, 2019. Online Edition. www.theglobeandmail.com/opinion/articlecanadas-political-institutions-are-failing-the-next-parliament-must/.

Segal, Edward. "How And Why Corporate Lobbying Will Continue to Matter During the Biden Administration." *Forbes*. January 26, 2021. Online Edition. www.forbes.com/sites/edwardsegal/2021/01/26/how-and-why-corporate-lobbying-will-continue-to-matter-during-the-biden-administration/?sh=140fb9f144dd.

Smith, Patrick. "Lobbying in Africa: Nightmare on K Street." *The Africa Report*. November 28, 2014. https://www.theafricareport.com/3674/lobbying-in-africa-nightmare-on-k-street/.

"Spiralling scandal: Voters do not think MPs should be allowed to profit from their job." Politics - Britain. *The Economist*. November 13th, 2021 Edition. www.economist.com/britain/2021/11/11/voters-do-not-want-mps-to-profit-from-their-job.

Teles, Steven and Mark Schmitt. "The Elusive Craft of Evaluating Advocacy." https://hewlett.org/wp-content/uploads/2016/08/Elusive_Craft.pdf. 2016.

"The Chamber of Secrets". Corporate Lobbying."

Business. *The Economist*. April 21st, 2012 Edition. https://www.economist.com/business/2012/0 4/21/the-chamber-of-secrets.

"The Great Embiggening". Briefing: State Spending. *The Economist*. November 20th, 2021 Edition. https://www.economist.com/briefing/2021/11 /20/governments-are-not-going-to-stop-getting-bigger.

"The New Order of Trade. Special Report: World Trade – October 9th 2021." *The Economist*, October 9th to 15th, 2021. https://www.economist.com/business/2021/0 5/13/the-power-of-lobbyists-is-growing-in-brussels-and-berlin.

"The power of lobbyists is growing in Brussels and Berlin." Business. *The Economist*. May 15, 2001.

Thibault, John. *How to Change a Law: The Intelligent Consumer's 7-Step Guide*. Menlo Park, California: iLobby, 2016.

Thurber, James. A. "Changing the Way Washington Works? Assessing President Obama's Battle with Lobbyists." https://www.american.edu/spa/ccps/upload/c hanging-the-way-washington-works_thurber.pdf.

Turmel, André, Guy Giorno and Pierre B. Meunier.

Lobbying in Canada/Lobbyisme au Canada. Toronto: Carswell, 2003.

United Nations. https://www.un.org/en/about-us/main-bodies.

Vance, Stephanie. *The Influence Game: 50 Insider Tactics from the Washington D.C. Lobbying World that Will Get You to Yes.* Hoboken, NJ: Wiley, 2012.

Watson, Iain and Patrick Clahane. "All-party groups: Calls for stronger anti-lobbying rules for MPs." *BBC News Online.* November 28, 2021. https://www.bbc.com/news/uk-politics-59416314.

Wills, Gary. *James Madison: The American Presidents.* New York: Times Books, 2002.

Zetter, Lionel. *Lobbying: The Art of Political Persuasion.* Petersfield, UK: Harriman House, 2014.

Henley Point Productions 2022

www.henleypoint.ca

www.ingramcontent.com/pod-product-compliance
Lightning Source LLC
Chambersburg PA
CBHW051125050326
40690CB00006B/807